Nita Mehta's

101 recipes for children

VEGETARIAN

Nita Mehta's 101 recipes for children

VEGETARIAN

VEGETARIAN

First published in 2010 by

Snab Publishers Pvt Ltd

Corporate Office
3A/3, Asaf Ali Road, New Delhi 110 002
Phone: +91 11 2325 2948, 2325 0091
Telefax: +91 11 2325 0091
E-mail: sales@snabindia.com
Website: www.snabindia.com

Editorial and Marketing office
E-159, Greater Kailash II, New Delhi 110 048
Phone: 91 11 2921 4011, 2921 8727, 2921 8574
Fax: +91 11 2922 5218, 2922 9558
E-mail: nitamehta@nitamehta.com
Website: www.nitamehta.com

Cover Design and Book Design by Rachna Panchal

Food Styling and Photography by Snab
Typesetting by National Information Technology Academy, 3A/3, Asaf Ali Road, New Delhi 110 002

Recipe Development & Testing:
Nita Mehta Foods - R & D Centre
3A/3, Asaf Ali Road, New Delhi - 110002
E-143, Amar Colony, Lajpat Nagar-IV, New Delhi - 110024

Distributed by : **NITA MEHTA BOOKS**
NITA MEHTA BOOKS
3A/3, Asaf Ali Road, New Delhi - 02

Distribution Centre :
D16/1, Okhla Industrial Area, Phase-I,
New Delhi - 110020
        Tel.: 26813199, 26813200
Bhogal: Tel.: 24372279

Printed by :
R P PRINTERS

© Copyright SNAB PUBLISHERS PVT LTD 2010

All rights reserved

ISBN 978-81-7869-263-0

Printed in India

WORLD RIGHTS RESERVED: The contents - all recipes, photographs and drawings are original and copyrighted. No portion of this book shall be reproduced, stored in a retrieval system or transmitted by any means, electronic, mechanical, photocopying, recording or otherwise, without the written permission of the publishers. While every precaution is taken in the preparation of this book, the publishers and the author assume no responsibility for errors or omissions. Neither is any liability assumed for damages resulting from the use of information contained herein.

TRADEMARKS ACKNOWLEDGED: Trademarks used, if any, are acknowledged as trademarks of their respective owners. These are used as reference only and no trademark infringement is intended upon. Ajinomoto (monosodium glutamade, MSG) is a trademark of Aji-no-moto company of Japan. Use it sparingly if you must as a flavour enhancer.

Price: Rs. 395/-

INTRODUCTION

Food provides nourishment for the healthy growth of a child but it also has a psychological aspect. The table can become a battle field. The parent can insist, "This is good for you," and the child can stubbornly say, "But I don't like it."

This book aims to give parents the choice to provide a healthy and nourishing diet, while respecting the right of the child to be a child - to have child-like cravings and preferences.

With a little wisdom and the right recipes, one can make food that is child-friendly in size, uncomplicated in taste, and fun to eat. The child does not have to become aware of the parent's 'hidden agenda' to cram in all the required proteins, carbohydrates, vitamins and minerals that promote strong bones, sustained energy, and all the building blocks required for the growth of body and brain.

The recipes in this book have been tried and tested on children of different ages. The final selection has been made by the children themselves.

The Tiffin Box items should look fresh and appetising and taste good too. Snacks should be like finger-food that little fingers can pick up with ease. Meal Time Dishes should be simple - but set a high standard that the child will learn to appreciate for the rest of his life. A special section on Sandwiches takes care of a hearty meal 'on-the-go', in the busy life of both mother and child. And every child deserves Sweet Delights, to share family celebrations, or just the joy of family life. Finally, Shakes, Smoothies and Ice Creams cater to the special cravings of teenagers.

We believe this book would give you the confidence to cook food that makes your kids happy, knowing that you have also selected the right ingredients that will make them healthy and strong.

ABOUT THE RECIPES
WHAT'S IN A CUP?
INDIAN CUP
1 teacup = 200 ml liquid

AMERICAN CUP
1 cup = 240 ml liquid (8 oz.)
The recipes in this book were tested with the Indian teacup which holds 200 ml liquid.

CONTENTS

TIFFIN BOX.....9

Carrot & Banana Wheat Muffins.....10
Cheese Balls.....12
Dalia Upma.....14
Oat-Moong Toast.....15
Sabodana Faces.....16
Crispy Aloo Dalia Tikki.....17
Chana Cheese Mix.....18
Quick Wheat Pasta.....19
Namkeen Seviyaan.....20
Baked Atta Mathis.....21
Paneer Kakori.....22
Nutritious Hara Chillah.....24

SNACKS.....25

Oat Hearts.....26
Veggie Cheese Slice.....27
Garlic Bread.....27
Raw Banana and Paneer Balls.....28
Healthy Onion Rings.....30
Stack it on a Cracker.....31
Paper Thin Veggie Chips.....32
Cheese & Garlic Pita Wedges.....33
Soya Bites.....35
Whole Wheat Nutty Goujons.....36
Mexican Antojitos Minis.....39
Crispy Cauliflower Rolls.....40
Sesame Potato Triangles.....42
Savoury Lollipops.....43
Grilled Cheesy Bites.....44
Mini Corn Buns.....47
Bread Pakora.....48
Khandvi.....49
Paneer Rolls.....50
Nutri Hearts.....51
Potato Shashlik.....52
Paneer Tikkas.....53
Vegetable Bread Patties.....54
Quick Bread Poha.....55
Dakshini Squares.....56
Vegetable Chaat Nuggets.....57
Quick Paneer Bites.....58
Hidden Veggie Pizza.....59
Kandhari Canapes.....60
Chilli Soya Bites.....61

MEAL TIME DISHES.....62

Mexican Quesadillas.....63
Kathi Nugget Rolls.....64
Macaroni.....65
Penne with Veggies.....66
Multigrain Wraps.....69
Kids Popeye Semolina Burgers.....70
Vegetable & Cheese Paranthas.....72
Protein Pulao.....73
Healthy Mixed Dal.....75
Lauki and Tomato Soup.....76
Karaari Arbi.....77
Pav Bhaji.....78
Pasta in Quick Tomato Sauce.....80
Instant Idli.....81
Paneer Makhani.....83
Sambar.....84
Vada.....85
Chilli Paneer Dosa.....86

SANDWICHES.....87

Veg. Club Sandwiches.....88
Peanut Butter Sandwiches.....89
Tikka Paneer Sandwiches.....90
Apple & Carrot Sandwiches.....91
Cheese-Raisin Sandwiches.....92
Green Peas Sandwiches.....93
Spinach & Corn Sandwiches.....94
Brown Veg. Sandwiches.....94
Vegetable Sandwiches.....96
Croquette Subwich.....97

SWEET DELIGHTS.....98

Spinach & Beetroot Cookies.....99
Date Fingers.....100
Oat Ka Halwa.....101
Caramel Popcorn.....102
Atta Laddu.....103
Jam Cookies.....104
Frozen Chocolate Bananas.....105
Sugar Coated Peanuts.....106
Pineapple Upside Down Cake.....107
Molten Choco Cup Cake.....108
Sweetheart Cookies.....110
Chocolate Biscuit Sticks.....111
Peanut Brownies.....113
Fruit and Jelly Wedges.....114
Fresh Fruit Kebabs.....114
Donuts.....115
Choco Cake.....116
Nan Khatai.....117
Fruity Chocolate Squares.....118
Jelly Custard.....119
Cinnamon Wheat Crispies.....120

SHAKES & ICE CREAM.....122

Yogurt Pops.....123
Mango Duet Ice Cream.....124
Apricot Almond Delight.....126
Orange Yogurt Ice Cream.....127
Fresh Chikoo Icecream.....128
Kesar Badam Milk.....129
Mango Mania.....130
Orange Rose Smoothie.....131
Breakfast Smoothie.....131
Nutty Banana Smoothie.....132
Strawberry Smoothie.....132

International Conversion Guide.....133
Herbs & Spices.....134

USEFUL TIPS

1. Some recipes require almond powder and soya bean powder. It is very handy if you make them into a powder and store them separately in air tight bottles (soya bean powder can be obtained by grinding the soya nutri nuggets). Add them to wheat flour while making dough for chappati.

2. When making french fries always make them without removing the peel of the potato.

3. Almond powder can be added to a glass of milk.

4. Always keep boiled potatoes, unpeeled in the refrigerator. They come handy when needed.

5. Palak paste can be made by blanching washed palak leaves and making a puree in the mixer. This can be kept covered in a container and refrigerated. This remains good for a week. It can be used in various recipes and saves a lot of time.

6. Puree any prepared vegetable (dry subzi) to a paste in a mixer. Knead it with wheat flour to a dough to make healthy vegetable chappatis.

7. Puree any fruit like strawberry, guava, grapes etc. with curd/ milk in a mixer to get healthy smoothies.

8. If your child refuses to eat vegetables, remember that fruit is the ideal substitute. Fruit supplies the same nutrients as vegetables, notably vitamins A and C, fibre and essential minerals such as potassium. Most children will happily tuck into a piece of fruit or cut-up portions with no worries.

9. Dalia can be roasted in a large quantity and kept in an air tight container.

Tiffin Box

A mother packs her child's tiffin box every day with love and care. When it comes back untouched she feels hurt and defeated. In this chapter learn to make irresistible tiffin food that will be greeted with joy, and gobbled up to the last crumb! Remember that the way the food is packed should also look very tempting.

Carrot & Banana Wheat Muffins

■ Attractive colourful speckles of carrots and raisins give these healthy whole wheat muffins the top prize!

makes 10-12 muffins

Ingredients
- 75 gm whole wheat flour (atta)
- 100 gm flour (maida)
- 1½ tsp baking powder
- ¾ tsp soda-bi-carb
- 75 gm (½ cup) yellow salted butter - softened
- 1 tsp vanilla essence
- 120 gm (1 cup) powdered sugar
- 2 large ripe bananas - pureed in a mixer (1 cup)
- 1 cup grated carrots
- 3 tbsp raisins (kishmish)

Method
1. Sieve the flours, baking powder and the soda-bi-carb.
2. Add carrots and raisins to the flour. Keep aside
3. Beat butter, essence and sugar till light and fluffy.
4. Add banana puree and beat well. Remove the beaters.
5. Add half of the flour and mix well. Add the remaining flour and mix to get a thick lumpy batter. Do not overmix. Just mix enough to moisten the dry ingredients.
6. Line a muffin pan (tray) with paper cups. Spoon mixture into them with an ice cream scooper, filling them ¾ only. (Even small steel katoris will do. Grease katoris and dust lightly with flour). Bake at 160°C for 20-25 minutes till golden on the top.

Cheese Balls

Mouth-watering golden balls bursting with flavour – learn the secret of making them feather-light and puffy.

Makes 20 balls

Ingredients

- 100 gm processed cheese - finely grated
- ¾ cup very hot milk
- 1 tsp yellow butter
- ¾ cup plain flour (maida)
- ¾ cup cornflour
- 1 tsp salt
- ½ tsp pepper
- ½ red chilli flakes
- ½ tsp raw cumin seeds (jeera) powder
- 2 tbsp chopped mint or coriander leaves
- 2 tbsp hung yogurt

  ADD AT FRYING TIME
- 1 tsp baking powder
- ½ tsp eno fruit salt
- oil for frying

Method

1. Finely grate cheese and add to hot milk in a bowl. Add butter. Mix with a whisk.
2. Sift flour and cornflour together. Add flour gradually to the milk, mixing well to get a soft dropping consistency. Add just enough flour to reach the right consistency.
3. Add salt, pepper, jeera powder and red chilli powder. Add mint or coriander and yogurt. Beat very well with an electric hand beater for 3 minutes. Keep aside till serving time. (You can refrigerate it upto 2-3 days.)
4. Add baking powder and eno at the time of frying.
5. Heat oil for frying till medium hot. Reduce heat. Put small portions of the mixture quickly into the oil with wet fingers. Put about 8-10 balls at a time. (Keep a bowl of water to dip fingers each time). Fry each batch for about 3 minutes on low medium heat, stirring constantly until they puff up and get cooked from inside. The colour is light golden, so keep frying on low heat till done and golden. The mixture can be fried in 2-3 batches, depending on the size of the kadhai but remember not to crowd the balls in the oil.
6. Serve with ketchup.

Dalia Upma

Lightly spiced, roasted dalia is tossed with colourful veggies and lifted with lemon juice and coriander leaves.

serves 4

Ingredients

- 1 cup roasted dalia (broken wheat)
- ¾ cup water
- 1 tbsp oil
- 1 tsp mustard seeds (rai)
- 1 small onion - chopped
- 1 potato - chopped
- 1 small carrot - chopped
- 1 tbsp green peas (matar)
- ½ capsicum - chopped
- 1 floret (a small piece) of cauliflower - chopped
- 1-2 french beans - chopped (optional)
- salt to taste
- 1½ cups water
- juice of ½ lemon
- 1 tbsp chopped coriander leaves

Method

1. Soak the dalia in ¾ cup water for half an hour.
2. Heat oil in a pan. Add mustard seeds, let them splutter for 30 seconds.
3. Add chopped onion. Stir for 1 minute.
4. Add potato, carrot, peas, capsicum, cauliflower and french beans, stir well for a minute.
5. Add salt. Cook covered on low flame till the potatoes get cooked.
6. Drain the water from the dalia and mix with the cooked vegetables. Stir for 3-4 minutes, then add 1½ cups water. Let it boil. Cover and cook on low flame for 3-4 minutes or till water is completely absorbed.
7. Add juice of half lemon and sprinkle coriander leaves on it. Serve hot.

Oat-Moong Toast

An unbelievable combination of taste and texture that is also good for your child's health.

serves 2

Ingredients

- ½ cup oats - roasted for 2 minutes in a kadhai
- ¼ cup dhuli Moong dal - soaked for 1-2 hours & ground to a paste
- ½ cup coriander leaves - chopped finely
- ½ tsp baking powder
- 1½ tsp lemon juice
- 1¼ tsp salt or to taste
- a pinch of red chilli powder
- 4-5 tbsp oil
- 4 slices of brown bread

Method

1. Drain and grind dal to a fine paste.
2. Mix moong dal paste, oats, coriander leaves, baking powder, lemon juice, salt and red chilli powder. Add enough water to make a paste.
3. Heat 4-5 tbsp oil in a non stick pan.
4. Spread the moong paste on one side of the bread slice with a spoon.
5. Invert the slice with the moong paste down in the hot oil.
6. Spread some moong paste on the upper side of the slice too, with a spoon. Turn. Shallow fry on both sides until light brown.
7. Remove from pan on to a paper napkin to absorb any excess oil.
8. Cut into two triangles.
9. Serve hot with tomato sauce or mint chutney.

Sabodana Faces

These deep-fried plump tikkis come alive with peppercorn eyes and ketchup smiles to make the children laugh with joy!

makes 12

Ingredients

- ½ cup sago (sabodana) - soak in ½ cup warm water for 2 hours
- 4 medium potatoes - boiled and mashed
- 2 tsp poppy seeds (khus khus)
- ½ cup cornflour
- 1 tsp chopped ginger
- 1 green chilli - chopped
- ½ tsp chaat masala
- 1 medium onion - chopped finely
- 2 tbsp chopped green coriander
- ½ tsp garam masala
- ½ tsp red chilli powder
- ½ tsp amchoor
- 1 tsp salt
- oil for frying
  DECORATION
- 10-12 whole pepper corns
- some tomato ketchup in a squeeze bottle

Method

1. Soak sabodana in about ½ cup warm water to cover it for 2-3 hours or till soft and spread on a plate.
2. Mix mashed potatoes and all the other ingredients, except pepper corns and ketchup. Mix well to get a tikki mixture.
3. Shape into 12 balls. Flatten each ball and press 2 pepper corns like two eyes.
4. Deep fry 2-3 pieces in a kadhai at a time in medium hot oil till golden.
5. Make a mouth shape with ketchup. Serve hot.

Crispy Aloo Dalia Tikki

Your kids and their friends are going to gobble up these mouth-size, high-fibre, kaju-flavoured tikkis!

makes 18

Ingredients

- ½ cup broken wheat (dalia)
- 2 boiled potatoes - peeled & mashed
- 1 cup finely chopped spinach
- 1 tsp finely chopped ginger
- 1 tbsp cashewnuts - powdered
- ½ cup milk
- ½ tsp salt or to taste
- ½ tsp garam masala
- oil for frying

Method

1. In a pan roast the dalia till golden in colour. Remove and soak in a bowl with ½ cup milk. Keep aside.
2. Mix the potatoes with the soaked dalia along with all the rest of the ingredients, except oil.
3. Divide the mixture into small equal portions. Make a ball of each portion and flatten between your palms in the shape of a small tikki.
4. Heat oil in a kadhai and deep fry 2-3 tikkis at a time till golden and crisp. Serve hot with tomato ketchup.

Chana Cheese Mix

■ Little fingers will want to play with these pieces – so let them! Then they will put the pieces into their mouths – such colourful bits and bites of healthy veggies and high-protein.

serves 4

Ingredients

- ½ cup chickpeas (safed chhole) - soaked overnight
- ½ cup chopped cucumber (kheera)
- ½ cup fresh pomegranate (anaar ke daane)
- 1 tsp chaat masala (optional)
- ½ tsp pepper
- ½ tsp salt or to taste
- 2 tbsp olive oil
- 2 cheese cubes - cut into smaller cubes

Method

1. Pressure cook channas with 2 cups water and 1 tsp salt. Cook till 1 whistle and then cook on slow flame for 15 minutes. Remove from fire. After the pressure drops, strain channa and keep aside to cool.
2. To serve mix all ingredients together in a bowl with the channas.

Quick Wheat Pasta

"Yum! This has so much lovely cheese!" The grated veggies are invisible in this creamy pasta dish!

serves 2-3

Ingredients
- 2 cups whole wheat fusilli pasta
- 1 tbsp butter
- 1 spring onion - chopped diagonally, keep greens separate
- 2 tsp cornflour dissolved in
- ½ cup milk
- 1 cup grated bottle gourd (ghiya) dudhi or zucchini
- ½ cup grated cauliflower
- ½ cup finely grated cheddar cheese
- ½ tsp salt
- ¼ tsp pepper

Method
1. To boil pasta, boil 6 cups water with 1 tsp salt. Add pasta and boil for 10-12 minutes till soft. Strain. Sprinkle 1 tbsp olive oil. Keep aside.
2. Heat butter in a non-stick pan, add the white of spring onion and saute for a minute. Add ghiya and cauliflower. Stir for 3-4 minutes.
3. Mix milk and cornflour. Add to the vegetables in the pan. Mix well.
4. Add cheese & pasta. Add greens of spring onions. Sprinkle salt and pepper & mix well. Serve immediately.

Namkeen Seviyaan

Children will enjoy the complex swirl of colours and the hearty and satisfying taste of this airy and light snack.

serves 4-5

Ingredients

- 200 gm vermicelli (seviyaan)
- 3 tsp butter or ghee
- ½ tsp cumin seeds (jeera)
- 1 onion - finely chopped
- seeds of 2 green cardamoms (chhoti elaichi) - crushed
- 1 cup chopped carrot
- 1 small capsicum - chopped
- ½ cup finely shredded spinach
- ¼ tsp garam masala
- 1 tsp salt
- ¼ tsp sugar
- 1 tsp lemon juice

Method

1. Boil 6 cups water in a pan with 1 tsp oil and 1 tsp salt. Add vermicelli. Cook for a minute. Drain. Drizzle 1 tbsp oil and mix. Keep aside.
2. In a pan heat butter or ghee. Add cumin seeds and stir for 30 seconds.
3. Add onions and crushed cardamoms and cook till onions are golden in colour.
4. Add carrot, capsicum and spinach. Cook for 4-5 minutes till carrots turn soft.
5. Add garam masala, salt and sugar. Mix.
6. Add vermicelli and lemon juice. Mix well. Serve.

Baked Atta Mathis

Here is an example that proves that baking can be used instead of frying even for traditional snacks, with excellent results.

makes 8

Ingredients
- ½ cup whole wheat flour (atta)
- ½ cup gram flour (besan)
- ¼ tsp turmeric (haldi) powder
- 1 tbsp dry fenugreek (kasoori methi) leaves or 3 tbsp chopped spinach leaves (paalak)
- 3 tbsp ghee
- pinch of asafoetida (hing)
- ½ tsp salt
- water as required

Method
1. Mix all the ingredients together and make a stiff dough by adding 3 tbsp water.
2. Make marble sized balls. Roll out into thin, small circles like papris. Prick them with a fork nicely.
3. Arrange them on a well greased baking tray and bake in a preheated hot oven at 150°C for 15-20 minutes or till done. Remove. Let them cool slightly.

Paneer Kakori

These vegetarian seekh kebabs are as silky soft as the famous kakoris. They are delicately flavoured with ground almonds – watch them disappear off the plate!

makes 15

Ingredients

- 100 gm paneer - crumbled or roughly mashed (1 cup)
- 2 medium potatoes - boiled and mashed
- 8-10 almonds - grind in mixer to a powder
- 2 tsp ginger-garlic paste
- 1 onion - very finely chopped
- 1 tsp bhuna jeera powder
- 1 tsp salt
- 1 tsp red chilli powder
- $\frac{1}{4}$ tsp amchoor
- 3 slices of bread - torn into pieces and churned in a mixer to get fresh crumbs
  INGREDIENTS FOR LATER USE
- 2 tbsp melted butter or oil
- tandoori or chaat masala
- onion rings
- lemon wedges

Method

1. Mix paneer, mashed potatoes, bread crumbs, almond powder and all other ingredients. Mix well to make a slightly stiff paste.
2. Rub oil generously on the wire rack or grill of the oven.
3. Take a lemon sized ball of the mixture and press the kebab mixture into finger-shaped kebabs on a pencil. Gently pull out the pencil to get a hole in the kebab.
4. Brush the kebabs with oil.
5. Place on a grill rack of the oven. Grill in a hot oven for about 8-10 minutes or till golden brown.
6. Pour some melted butter on the kebabs with a tsp to baste them. Turn them only when they are almost done otherwise they tend to break. Spoon some butter on the other side also and grill for 5 minutes or till golden from both sides.
7. Sprinkle tandoori or chaat masala on the kebabs and serve with onion rings sprinkled with lemon juice and chaat masala and lemon wedges.

Note

If you do not wish to grill the kebabs, shallow fry in 1 tbsp oil in a pan, turning sides till browned evenly.

Nutritious Hara Chillah

Pancake power packed with nutrition, texture and taste! The pancake (chilla) is made with soaked ground green moong dal.

makes 10

Ingredients
- 1 cup hari tukda moong chilka
- 2 tsp chopped garlic
- ¼ cup chopped coriander leaves
- ½ tsp salt
- ¼ tsp garam masala
- ½ tsp coriander powder
- 1 cup water

TOPPING
- 2 carrots - finely grated (1 cup)
- 2 cups grated paneer
- 1½ tsp salt, or to taste
- 1 tsp roasted cumin (bhuna jeera) powder

Method
1. Wash dal well. Soak dal in 2 cups of water for 1-2 hours.
2. Drain dal.
3. Grind dal to a paste along with garlic, coriander, salt, garam masala and coriander powder in a mixer. Add 1 cup water. Grind again. Remove from mixer to a bowl.
4. Mix all ingredients of the topping in a bowl. Keep aside.
5. Grease a non-stick pan and heat on fire. Remove from fire and pour one karchhi of batter and immediately spread with the back of a karchhi into a 5" diameter round. Return to fire. Let it cook for a few seconds.
6. Sprinkle 2 tbsp of the topping on the chillah. Press.
7. Pour 1 tsp ghee/oil on the sides and on top too, so that the chillah turns crispy. When you see golden brown patches, turn over. Cook till golden from both sides. Serve hot.

Snacks

Can your snacks win the competition against chocolate bars and crisps? To meet this challenge of the age, get inspiration from the recipes in this chapter. Hey! Be cool with youth appeal!

Oat Hearts

When boiled potatoes are enriched with oats and paneer the nutrition angle is taken care of. Add great flavour and texture in an unusual heart shape and you have the perfect recipe for success.

serves 6-8

Ingredients

- 1½ cups oats
- 2 potatoes - boiled and mashed
- ¼ cup grated paneer
- ¾ tsp salt or to taste
- ¼ tsp red chilli powder
- ¼ tsp garam masala
- ½ tsp amchoor
- 2 tbsp chopped coriander leaves
- ¼ cup grated carrot
- ¼ tsp lemon juice
- oil for frying

Method

1. Keep ½ cup oats aside for coating.
2. Mix all the other ingredients with 1 cup oats.
3. Make 8-10 balls of the above mixture.
4. Flatten each ball and shape into hearts or cut with a heart shape cookie cutter. Do not flatten too much.
5. Spread the remaining ½ cup oats on a plate. Dip each heart in a bowl of water for a second & immediately press both sides of each heart in oats. Press hearts with the palms to make the oats coat properly.
6. To pan fry the hearts, heat 2-3 tbsp oil in a pan. Fry 3-4 hearts at a time. When the underside turns golden, turn. Fry this side for a few minutes. Remove from oil and serve with ketchup.

Veggie Cheese Slice

A cheesy topping and finely diced, crunchy veggies, flavoured with basil, oregano and mustard – the grown-ups will beg the kiddies for one more bite!

makes 3-4

Ingredients
- 1 small french loaf or bread
- 2 tbsp butter

TOPPING
- ¾ cup grated cheddar cheese
- 2 tbsp finely chopped onions
- 2 tbsp finely chopped capsicum
- 2 tbsp finely chopped deseeded tomato (cut a tomato into 4 pieces and remove pulp)
- 2 tbsp corn kernels
- 1 tbsp olive oil or cream
- 4-5 fresh basil leaves - roughly torn or 2 tbsp chopped coriander leaves
- ½ tsp chilli flakes
- ½ tsp oregano, ¼ tsp pepper
- a pinch of salt
- 1 tsp mustard paste

Method
1. Cut the french bread into 1" thick diagonal slices. Apply butter and grill with the buttered side up till golden brown.
2. Mix all the ingredients of the topping lightly in a bowl. Pile the topping on the untoasted side of the bread. Place bread under a grill for 3-4 minutes and grill till cheese melts. Serve immediately.

Garlic Bread

Did you ever wonder what makes garlic bread so delicious? This recipe gives you all the secrets to achieve perfection.

serves 8

Ingredients
- 1 French loaf
- 1½ cups grated mozzarella cheese
- 1 tbsp olive oil

GARLIC SPREAD
- 6 tbsp olive oil or softened butter
- 2-4 crushed flakes of garlic
- a pinch salt, ¼ tsp pepper
- ½ tsp red chilli flakes
- ½ tsp oregano

Method
1. Cut the loaf into ½" thick slices.
2. To prepare the spread, mix all the ingredients of spread in a small bowl.
3. Put the garlic spread on all the pieces of the bread.
4. Mix cheese with 1 tbsp olive oil. Sprinkle some cheese on each piece of bread.
5. To serve, bake in a preheated oven at 200°C for 10-15 minutes or till the bread turns crisp.

Raw Banana and Paneer Balls

Bananas are rich in calcium and potassium. Alongwith cottage cheese, they make a wonderful healthy snack for children.

Makes 16 balls

Ingredients

- 200 gms paneer - grated
- 2 kacha kela (raw banana)
- 2 tsp green chilli paste
- 2 tsp ginger paste
- ¾ tsp salt, or to taste
- 6 tsp whole wheat flour (atta)
- 4 tsp coarsely powdered peanuts
- 2 tbsp fresh coriander leaves
- oil for frying

Method

1. Wash bananas with the peel. Put in a poly bag. Microwave bananas along with the peel for 3 minutes. Peel and mash well.
2. Mix all ingredients well and shape into small balls.
3. Deep fry in hot oil till golden brown. Serve hot with chutney.

Healthy Onion Rings

A well-flavoured batter combines with the sweet taste of onions in a size and shape that keeps little fingers and mouths busy and satisfied.

makes 4-6

Ingredients

- 2-3 large onions
  BATTER
- ¼ cup atta (whole wheat flour)
- ¼ cup cornflour
- ¼ tsp garlic paste
- 1 tsp lemon juice
- ½ tsp each salt, pepper and oregano
- a pinch of red chilli flakes

Method

1. Cut onion into thick slices. Separate slices to get rings. Dip them in cold water and keep aside for ½ hour.
2. Make a thick coating batter with all the ingredients of the batter. Mix well. (No lumps should remain.) Keep aside for 10 minutes.
3. Drain the onion rings. Wipe the onion rings dry on a kitchen towel.
4. Heat oil. Dip onion rings in the batter and deep fry 5-6 pieces at a time till golden in colour and crisp. Remove from oil & drain on paper napkins. Repeat with all the rings.
5. Serve with tomato ketchup.

Tip
Whole baby corn, whole mushrooms or capsicum rings fried this way make an excellent snack.

Stack it on a Cracker

This cheerful presentation packs loads of nutrition with soya nuggets, spinach and cheese.

makes 8

Ingredients

- 3 cheese slices
- 2 tbsp cheese spread
- 12 crackers

  TOPPING
- ¼ cup soya nutri granules
- 1 tbsp oil
- 2 tbsp finely chopped onion
- 2 tbsp finely chopped spinach (palak)
- ¾ tsp salt
- ½ tomato - chopped finely
- 2 tbsp grated boiled potato

Method

1. Boil ½ cup water in a pan and add the granules; leave for 20 minutes. Strain and squeeze nicely.
2. Heat oil in a pan. Add onions and saute for 1 minute. Add the spinach and cook till all the moisture dries.
3. Add the drained soya granules and salt, saute for 2 minutes. Add the tomato and cook for a minute.
4. Remove from flame and mix the mashed potatoes with the granules. Keep topping aside.

TO ASSEMBLE THE CRACKERS

1. Cut each cheese slice into 4 square pieces.
2. On a cracker, place a square cheese at an angle leaving the edges (diamond shape).
3. Divide the topping into 12 parts. Place a portion of topping on the cracker with cheese single.
4. Dot it with cheese spread and tomato ketchup.

Paper Thin Veggie Chips

All kinds of root vegetables may be finely sliced and deep fried to make 'chips'. Serve as an accompaniment to a meal or simply by themselves as a nibble.

serves 4

Ingredients
- 2 carrots (gajar)
- 1 beetroot (chukunder)
- 1 sweet potato or potato
- oil for deep frying
- ¼ tsp pepper
- 1 tsp salt, ½ tsp oregano
- 2 tbsp cornflour

Method
1. Peel all the vegetables, then slice the carrot, beetroot and sweet potato with the help of peeler into thin long slices. Pat dry all the vegetables on kitchen paper.
2. Heat oil in a kadhai. Sprinkle veggies with cornflour and mix gently. This absorbs only excess moisture. Add the vegetable slices in batches and deep-fry for 2-3 minutes, until golden and crisp. Remove and drain on kitchen towels.
3. Immediately sprinkle pepper, oregano and salt over the hot chips.
4. Pile up the vegetable 'chips' on a serving plate and serve immediately.

Cheese & Garlic Pita Wedges

■ A readymade bread base saves time to make this crisp easy-to-hold snack that taste like every child's dream delight – pizza.

makes 16 wedges

Ingredients

- 1 whole wheat pita bread or 1 thick pizza base
- 6 tbsp melted butter
- 2 flakes of garlic - crushed (½ tsp)
- 3 tbsp chopped fresh basil or 1 tsp oregano
- ½ cup grated mozzarella or pizza cheese
- a pinch of salt & pepper

Method

1. Slit pita bread/pizza base horizontally from the centre to get 2 thin rounds.
2. Cut each pita bread/pizza base round equally into 8 wedges (triangular pieces). This way you have 16 pieces in all.
3. Combine butter, garlic, basil, salt and pepper, brush over inner/cut side of bread wedges, then sprinkle with mozzarella cheese.
4. Place in single layer on oven trays.
5. Bake in a hot oven for 5-6 minutes at 200°C or until crisp.

Soya Bites

Mini seekh kebabs cleverly fashioned with soya nuggets, herbs and spices are deep-fried for a perfect high-protein snack.

serves 4-6

Ingredients

- 2 medium potatoes - boiled and mashed
- ¼ cup nutri nugget soya granules - boiled in hot water for 5 minutes strained & squeezed
- 3 tbsp oil
- 1 tsp cumin seeds (jeera)
- 1 tsp ginger-garlic paste
- (½" ginger and 3-4 flakes garlic)
- 1 onion - chopped
- ¼ tsp turmeric (haldi)
- ½ tsp red chilli powder
- ½ tsp garam masala
- 1 tsp coriander (dhania) powder
- ¼ tsp dry mango powder (amchoor)
- ¾ tsp salt
- 3 tbsp tomato puree
- 1 tbsp cornflour
- 1-2 tsp lemon juice or to taste
- 1 bread slice - grind in a mixer to get fresh crumbs
- some satay sticks or bamboo skewers

Method

1. Heat 3 tbsp oil. Add 1 tsp cumin seeds. Let them turn golden.
2. Add ginger-garlic paste. Stir for a few seconds. Add onion. Cook on low heat till light brown.
3. Remove from fire and add masalas - turmeric, garam masala, red chilli powder, coriander powder, amchoor powder and salt. Stir to mix.
4. Return to fire and add tomato puree. Stir to mix.
5. Add nuggets and stir for about 10 minutes till well fried and absolutely dry. Remove from fire. Cool.
6. Mash the nuggets well. Add mashed potatoes, cornflour and bread crumbs. Add lemon and seasoning to taste.
7. Flatten a ball of this mixture on a wooden skewer. Do not make it too broad as the mixture might fall off.
8. Deep fry to serve. Serve with ketchup.

Whole Wheat Nutty Goujons

Goujons are deep-fried strips of chicken or fish but here potato fingers have been used instead. Deliciously flavoured with ground almonds, they are bound to appeal to grown-ups and kids alike.

serves 4

Ingredients

- 3-4 big potatoes - cut into thin fingers
- ½ tsp pepper
- 1 tsp salt
- ¼ cup almonds - powdered in a mixer
- 2½ cups fresh brown bread crumbs mixed with 4 tbsp plain flour (maida)
- 2 tsp finely chopped coriander leaves
- ½ tsp salt
- oil for deep frying

BATTER
- ¼ cup whole wheat flour (atta)
- 10 tbsp cold milk
- ¼ tsp salt

Method

1. Mix potato fingers with pepper and salt in a large bowl.
2. Put about 5 slices of brown bread broken into pieces in a grinder. Grind to get about 2½ cups fresh crumbs.
3. Mix together almond powder, 2½ cups bread crumbs, salt and coriander leaves in a bowl. Keep aside.
4. Mix all ingredients of the batter in a bowl. Mix well.
5. Now dip the potato finger in wheat flour batter and immediately roll into the bread crumb mixture to coat it completely. Chill in the freezer for 15-20 minutes.
6. Heat the oil in a pan and then deep fry the breaded potato sticks until golden brown. Drain on paper napkins and serve hot.

Mexican Antojitos Minis

These antojitos (Spanish for 'cravings') are appetizers that will be appreciated by all age groups. The little tortilla cups can be made in advance. To serve, just fill and grill!

makes 20

Ingredients
- 4 whole wheat flour tortillas
- ½ cup cheddar cheese
- ½ cup mozzarella or pizza cheese
- ½ cup corn kernels
- 1 red or yellow capsicum - chopped
- 2 green onions (hara pyaz) - chopped with the greens
- a pinch of salt and pepper
- muffin pan

Method
1. Preheat oven to 200°C.
2. Lightly grease the muffin pan.
3. Cut each tortilla into 5 round pieces with a big cookie cutter or a big katori. The cutter should be larger than the muffin cup so that you can get folds in the tortilla cups.
4. Lightly grease all tortilla rounds. Fit the pieces into the muffin cups, getting folds because these are bigger than the cups.
5. Grill for 5-7 minutes or until crisp. Store in an air tight box till serving.
6. To serve, mix both cheeses, corn, capsicum, green onions, salt and pepper in a bowl.
7. Sprinkle equal amount of filling into each baked tortilla cups.
8. Grill in the pre-heated oven for 5 minutes or until the cheeses turns light golden. Serve dotted with mayonnaise or ketchup.

Crispy Cauliflower Rolls

Oval balls or rolls, made with finely minced cauliflower and breadcrumbs are shallow-fried till crisp and golden. Serve them in a garlic-flavoured Chinese-style sauce.

makes 12

Ingredients

- 2 cups very finely chopped cauliflower (minced)
- 2 slices bread
- 2 tbsp plain flour (maida)
- 2 tbsp cornflour
- ½ tbsp rice flour, optional
- 1 tsp chilli powder
- ½ tsp pepper powder
- pinch of baking soda
- ½ tsp salt
- oil for frying

SAUCE
- 1 tbsp oil
- 12 flakes garlic - finely chopped (1 tbsp)
- 1 small onion - finely chopped
- 1 small capsicum - finely chopped
- ¼ cup hot sweet sauce or tomato ketchup
- ½ tsp soya sauce
- ½ tsp salt
- ¼ cup water

Method

1. Soak the bread slice in water for a second. Squeeze out the water and crumble into a large bowl. Add cauliflower, plain flour, cornflour, rice flour if available, chilli powder, pepper, baking soda and salt into the bowl and mix well. Sprinkle 1-2 tsp water if needed to form balls.

2. Make oval balls of about 1" length. You will need to press the balls well with the fingers so that they bind properly.

3. Heat oil for frying. Fry 2-3 pieces at a time on medium or low heat till crisp and deep brown. Drain on paper napkins.

4. For the sauce, heat oil in a pan. Reduce heat and add garlic. Stir. Add onion and capsicum and saute for 1 minute. Add hot and sweet sauce, soya sauce, and salt. Add ¼ cup water. Mix well. Remove from heat.

5. At the time of serving, heat the sauce, mix the rolls with the sauce and serve immediately.

Sesame Potato Triangles

■ These sesame-coated triangles are piled high with a potato-peas mixture & grilled. How do the peas taste so sweet? Find the secret in this recipe.

serves 4

Ingredients

- 4 slices of bread
- ¼ cup peas - fresh or frozen
- 2 medium potatoes - boiled and mashed
- ½ cup grated mozzarella cheese
- a big pinch of baking powder
- ½ tsp salt and a pinch of sugar
- ½ tsp crushed black pepper
- 1 tbsp sesame seeds (til)

Method

1. Lightly toast bread slices in a toaster and keep aside.
2. Boil 2 cups water with a pinch of sugar and ½ tsp salt. Add peas and boil for 2-4 minutes till soft. Strain. Cool and grind in mixer roughly.
3. Mix mashed potatoes to peas. Add grated cheese, baking powder, salt and pepper.
4. Mix well to get a soft paste. Check seasoning and keep the salt a little extra as it has to be spread on bread.
5. Spread mixture over each toasted bread slice and cut each bread slice into 2 triangles. Sprinkle sesame seeds generously. Press lightly with the fingers.
6. Place bread on a grill rack in a hot oven. Grill for 5 minutes till golden from the sides. Serve hot.

Savoury Lollipops

■ Clever mothers camouflage fibre-rich food in the shape of a chid's favourite candy - a lollipop!

serves 8

Ingredients

- 6 ice cream sticks or wooden spoons
- ½ cup kale channe - soaked and boiled with just enough water
- 2 potatoes - boiled
- 2 slices of bread (preferably brown bread) - crumbled
- 1 tbsp tomato ketchup
- 1 tsp salt
- ½ tsp garam masala
- ½ tsp red chilli powder
- ¼ tsp amchoor
- oil for frying

Method

1. Pressure cook kale channe till soft. If there is any water left, cook on fire till almost dry. Remove from fire and cool. Grind the channas to a paste.
2. Break bread into pieces and put in a mixer. Grind to get fresh bread crumbs.
3. Mix boiled potatoes, bread crumbs, ketchup, salt, garam masala, red chilli powder and amchoor to taste.
4. Make balls and insert a stick in each.
5. Flatten the ball on the stick.
6. Shallow-fry in a pan, one at a time, till golden along with the stick in hot oil.

Grilled Cheesy Bites

■ A child-friendly, small-sized bread base has a rich cheesy topping, scattered with multicoloured gems – tiny cubes of veggies.

serves 6-8

Ingredients

- 1 small french loaf or bread
- 2 tbsp olive oil, chilli flakes and oregano to sprinkle
  TOPPING
- ½ cup grated cheddar cheese
- ½ cup grated paneer
- 4 tbsp mayonnaise
- 2 tsp mustard paste
- 2 tsp tomato ketchup
- ½ tsp chilli flakes
- ½ tsp oregano, ¼ tsp pepper
- 2 pinches of salt
- 1 onion - chopped finely
- ½ green capsicum - chopped finely
- 1 small tomato - deseeded & finely chopped
  (cut a tomato into 4 pieces
  & remove pulp)
- ¼ cup chopped cabbage
- 2 tbsp chopped coriander leaves
- 2 tbsp corn kernels, optional

Method

1. Cut the french bread into ½" thick slices. Brush with olive oil. Sprinkle red chili flakes and oregano. Grill with the oil side up for anbout 4 minutes till golden brown.
2. Mix together cheese, paneer, mayonnaise, mustard, ketchup, salt, pepper, chilli flakes and oregano.
3. Add all the other ingredients of the topping and mix lightly.
4. Pile the topping on the untoasted side of the bread.
5. Place bread under a grill for 3-4 minutes and grill till light golden. Serve immediately.

Mini Corn Buns

■ Mini buns for little hands to hold with confidence, and a delicious mix of cheese, paneer and veggies to fill hungry stomachs!

makes 12

Ingredients

- 12 mini buns
- 2 tbsp olive oil mixed with $\frac{1}{4}$ tsp salt, pepper, oregano & pepper
- 2 tbsp oil
- 1 onion - finely chopped
- $\frac{3}{4}$ cup chopped cabbage
- $\frac{1}{2}$ red capsicum - cubed
- $\frac{1}{2}$ cup frozen corn
- 1 cheese cube - cut into tiny pieces
- $\frac{1}{2}$ cup tiny pieces of paneer
- 1 tbsp chopped coriander or
  1 tsp chopped mint or parsley
  MIX TOGETHER
- 3 tbsp mayonnaise
- 3 tbsp thick yogurt
- 2 tsp tomato ketchup
- 2 tsp chilli garlic spread

Method

1. Hollow out the buns. Brush the outside and inside of each bun with olive oil mixed with spices. Keep aside.
2. Heat 2 tbsp olive oil or regular cooking oil. Add onion and cook till soft. Add cabbage and cook for 3 minutes. Add red capsicum and corn. Mix well. Add $\frac{3}{4}$ tsp salt, $\frac{1}{2}$ tsp pepper and $\frac{1}{2}$ tsp oregano. Add coriander leaves, paneer and cheese. Mix well and keep aside.
3. Mix mayonnaise with thick yogurt, ketchup and chilli garlic spread.
4. Add vegetables to mayonnaise mix and check salt. Stuff in the buns and grill in a oven on the rack for 5 minutes till edges start to turn golden. Serve hot.

Bread Pakora

Sandwiched slices of bread coated with besan. If you like you can simply dip the bread slices in the besan batter and make besan waale toasts - a favourite of my son when he was a small child. He now heads this publishing house. Those crisp besan-coated toasts remind me of those wonderful years!

serves 3

Ingredients

- 6 slices of bread
  BATTER
- 1 cup gram flour (besan)
- ¾ - 1 cup water
- ½ tsp garam masala
- ½ tsp red chilli powder
- ½ tsp haldi, 1 tsp salt

FILLING
- 2 potatoes (aloos) - boiled, peeled and grated
- ¼ tsp red chilli powder, ¼ tsp amchoor
- ¼ tsp roasted cumin (bhuna jeera) powder
- ½ tsp dhania powder, ½ tsp salt
- 2 tbsp chopped onion
- 1 green chilli - deseeded & chopped

Method

1. Mix all the ingredients of batter in a flat dish. Mix well with a balloon whisk or a karcchi to break all the lumps.
2. Mix all ingredients of filling in a bowl. Divide the filling into 6 portions.
3. Cut each bread slice into 2 triangles. Spread 1 portion of filling on each bread. Press filling with fingers. Put the other triangle piece of bread on it. Press well to stick together.
4. Heat 5-6 tbsp oil in a non stick pan or add ½ cup oil in a kadhai.
5. Dip the sandwiched bread in the batter, immediately put it in the oil.
6. Shallow fry the bread on both sides until light brown. Drain on paper napkin. Serve hot with sauce.

Khandvi

This microwave method saves time. The finger-size cylinders of khandvi have a touch of sweetness in the garnish of fresh, grated coconut.

serves 6-8

Ingredients

- ½ cup besan
- 1¾ cups butter milk (mix ¾ cup curd with 1 cup water)
- ¼ tsp haldi
- ¼ tsp jeera
- ½ tsp coriander powder
- a pich hing
- 1 tsp salt, ½ tsp sugar
- 1 big (12") thali or tray - greased with oil

PASTE
- ½ inch piece ginger
- 1-2 green chillies
- TEMPERING
- 1½ tbsp oil, ½ tsp rai
- 2-3 green chillies
- few coriander leaves
- few curry leaves
- FILLING
- 2-3 tbsp freshly grated coconut
- 2 tbsp finely grated carrot

Method

1. Mix besan with buttermilk in a flat dish till smooth. Microwave uncovered for 4 minutes. Stir. Add all other ingredients and ginger-green chilli paste and microwave for 4 minutes. Stir and microwave for 2 minutes or until mixture becomes thick and translucent.
2. Spread mixture thinly on back of a greased tray or a thick plastic sheet put on the kitchen platform while it is hot. Immediately level it thinly with the help of a greased flat spoon.
3. Cut into 1½-2" wide strips and 7 inches long. Sprinkle coconut and carrot. Roll each strip to get small cylinders.
4. Mix all ingredient of tempering and microwave for 3 minutes. Pour it on the khandvis.

Paneer Rolls

Just the right size of finger food for little fingers. Watch them gobble up healthy protein and ask for more!

serves 4

Ingredients

- 200 gms paneer - grated
- ½ cup coriander leaves - finely chopped
- 1 cube cheese - grated
- 1 tbsp wheat flour (atta)
- 1 bread - dipped in water and squeezed
- ½ tsp ground cumin (jeera) powder
- ½ tsp salt or to taste
- oil for frying

Method

1. Mix all the ingredients except oil.
2. Make small elongated balls and shape them into 1½"-2" rolls.
3. Deep fry in hot oil till golden.
4. Remove from oil and serve with chutney.

Nutri Hearts

The familiar taste of maggie noodles; a new shape that grabs attention; the goodness of soya and almonds – this snack comes First in class!

serves 4

Ingredients

- 1 packet maggie masala noodles
- 2 tbsp butter
- 2 tbsp whole wheat flour (atta)
- ¾ cup milk
- 1 carrot - grated (¾ cup)
- ¾ cup finely chopped cabbage
- 1 tbsp nutri nugget powder (grind nutri granules)
- 1 tbsp almond powder (8-10 almonds, ground)
- salt and pepper to taste

Method

1. Boil maggie noodles in just 1 cup water on medium flame till the water gets absorbed.
2. Melt butter in a heavy bottomed kadahi on low heat.
3. Add atta and stir fry for 1 minute. Add milk stirring continuously.
4. Add carrots, cabbage, nutri nugget powder, almond powder and cook till thick.
5. Add salt and boiled maggie. Cook for 2-3 minutes more and keep mixing the noodles gently till the mixture turns really thick. Do not mash the noodles.
6. Cook till the mixture turns thick enough to be shaped into cutlets. Remove from fire. Cool. With oiled hands, make heart shaped cutlets and refrigerate overnight. Next morning shallow or deep fry them.

Potato Shashlik

Deep-fried potato balls are presented on toothpicks between red and green veggies to make shashliks that are smothered in a garlicky hot sauce.

serves 3

Ingredients

POTATO BALLS
- 1 cup boiled and mashed potatoes
- ½ tsp red chilli powder
- ¼ tsp bhuna jeera powder
- ½ tsp salt, ½ tsp chaat masala
- 2 bread slices - grind in a mixer to get 1 cup fresh bread crumbs

FOR SHASHLIK
- 1 green capsicum - cut into ½" triangle
- 1 firm small tomato - cut into 4 pieces and deseed, cut each piece into 2 pieces
- a few bamboo skewers or tooth picks

FOR SAUCE
- 1 tbsp oil, 1 tsp chopped garlic
- 1 tsp soya sauce, 1 tsp vinegar
- 2-3 tbsp tomato ketchup
- ¼ tsp salt
- ¼ tsp crushed black pepper

Method

1. For potato balls, take a bowl and mix all the ingredients of potato balls.
2. Make small marble size balls of this mixture. Deep fry till golden brown. Drain on paper. Keep aside.
3. For the sauce, mix soya sauce, tomato ketchup, salt, black pepper and vinegar in a bowl and keep aside.
4. Heat oil in a pan. Reduce heat and add chopped garlic and cook for a few seconds. Add all the ingredients collected in the bowl. Cook for a few seconds.
5. Add capsicum and tomatoes and cook for 1 minute on low flame. Remove from fire.
6. Add the fried potato balls in the sauce. Mix lightly.
7. On a wooden skewer, first thread a piece of capsicum, then a potato ball and finally a piece of tomato. Serve.

Paneer Tikkas

■ Paneer tikkas are soaked in creamy yogurt and cashew paste. Roasted besan gives a unique crisp coating. Tikkas are so easy for children to gobble up fast!

serves 4

Ingredients

- 200 gm paneer - cut into 1½" pices of 1" thickness
  GRIND TOGETHER
- 1 dried, whole red chilli - soaked in water for 10 minutes and drained
- 1" piece ginger, 5-6 flakes garlic
  MARINADE
- ½ cup yogurt - hang in a muslin cloth for 1 hour
- 2 tbsp thick malai or thick cream
- 2 tbsp kasoori methi - roast and and crush to a powder (2 tsp)
- a few drops of orange food colour or a pinch of turmeric (haldi)
- 1 tbsp mustard oil
- 1 tbsp roasted besan
- ½ tsp dried mango powder (amchoor)
- ½ tsp black salt (kala namak)
- ¾ tsp salt, or to taste
- 1 tbsp tandoori masala or barbecue masala
- 2 tbsp cashews - microwave with ¼ cup water for ½ minute, drain & grind to a fine paste

Method

1. Hang yogurt in a muslin cloth for 1 hour. Drain soaked red chilli. Grind ginger, garlic and red chilli to a paste.
2. To the ginger-garlic-chilli paste, add hung yogurt, cream or malai, kasoori methi, food colour or turmeric, 1 tbsp mustard oil, 1 tbsp besan, amchoor, black salt, salt, tandoori masala and cashew paste.
3. Add paneer to this marinade. Mix well.
4. Cover the wire rack of the oven with aluminium foil and grease with oil. Arrange paneer on it. At the time of serving, preheat the grill for 10 minutes. Put the paneer pieces on the wire rack in the hot oven. Grill for about 8-10 minutes. Sprinkle some oil on the paneer pieces. Change side if required. Grill for another 5 minutes. Serve immediately.

Vegetable Bread Patties

■ Sliced bread is a shortcut to making these quick and easy patties filled with cooked diced vegetables.

makes 4

Ingredients
- 4 slices bread
- 4-5 French beans - finely chopped
- 1 potato - finely chopped (½ cup)
- ¼ cup peas, 1 carrot - finely chopped
- 2 tbsp oil, ½ tsp finely chopped ginger
- 2 tbsp chopped coriander leaves
- 1 tsp salt, ¼ tsp red chilli powder
- ½ tsp pepper
- 1 tsp lemon juice
- oil for frying

Method
1. Heat oil. Add ginger. When it turns golden, add vegetables and cook covered for 5-7 minutes till done. Occasionally sprinkle water, to prevent the vegetables from burning.
2. Add finely chopped coriander leaves, salt, red chilli powder and pepper. Cook for ½ minute on low heat. Remove from heat. Add lemon juice and mix well. Cool the mixture.
3. Cut the sides of a bread slice. Dip the slice in water kept in a flat bowl and remove from water immediately. Keep it flat on the palm.
4. Press bread carefully, keeping it flat on the palm, to squeeze out water.
5. Put 1 tbsp of prepared vegetables in the centre of the wet bread. Cover with the sides of bread. Press well to give it a neat shape and seal on all sides by pressing.
6. At serving time, deep fry in hot oil to a light brown colour. As soon as the patty is put in oil, do not touch it with the frying spoon immediately to avoid sticking. Turn after a while when it starts to change colour. Fry 2-3 pieces at a time. Drain on paper. Serve hot with tomato ketchup.

Quick Bread Poha

■ Two options – paneer or channa – are given for this quick and filling snack tossed together with bread squares.

serves 1-2

Ingredients

- 2 brown bread slices - cut into 1" square pieces
- 2 tbsp peas or corn kernels
- 1 onion - chopped
- 1 firm tomato - chopped
- ¼ cup paneer/boiled channa
- ½ potato - boiled & cubed
- ¼ tsp mustard seeds (rai)
- a few curry leaves
- a pinch of turmeric (haldi)
- salt to taste
- 2 tbsp oil

Method

1. Heat 2 tbsp oil in a pan. Add mustard seeds and curry leaves. Wait for 30 seconds.
2. Add onion. Stir for a minute. Add salt and haldi. Mix. Add potatoes. Stir for 2 minutes. Add peas and tomato. Cook for 2 minutes.
3. Add paneer or channas. Mix well.
4. Add the bread squares to the mixture. Mix well and serve hot.

Dakshini Squares

This toast topping is flavoured with curry leaves and mustard seeds. Gentle shallow frying is required to bring out the best. A brilliant answer to a child's hunger and curiosity.

serves 4

Ingredients
- 1 cup boiled and grated potatoes (2 potatoes)
- 2 tbsp semolina (suji)
- ½ tsp salt, or to taste
- ¼ tsp pepper, or to taste
- ½ onion - very finely chopped
- ½ tomato - cut into half, deseeded and chopped finely
- 2 tbsp curry leaves
- 3 bread slices - toasted in a toaster
- ½ tsp small brown mustard seeds (rai)
- 3 tsp oil to shallow fry

Method
1. Mix the suji, salt and pepper with the boiled potatoes.
2. Add the onion, tomato and curry leaves.
3. Spread potato mixture carefully on toasted bread slices, keeping edges neat.
4. Sprinkle some rai over the potato mixture, pressing down gently with finger tips.
5. Heat 1 tsp oil in a non stick pan. Add a slice of bread with topping side down.
6. Cook until the topping turns golden brown and crisp. Add a little more oil for the next slice if required. Cut each slice into 4 pieces and serve hot.

Note

This recipe will work best using a minimum quantity of oil for frying.

Vegetable Chaat Nuggets

Delicious and soft nuggets with a crisp covering, similar in taste to the pao bhaji mixture.

serves 4

Ingredients

- 1 cup chopped cabbage
- 1 cup chopped cauliflower (tiny florets)
- ½ cup shelled peas
- 2 potatoes - boiled and grated
- ½ cup very finely chopped carrots
- 3 tbsp oil
- 1 tsp ginger-garlic paste
- 2½ tsp pao-bhaji masala
- 2 bread slices- churned in a mixer to get fresh crumbs
- ¾ tsp salt, or to taste, ½ tsp sugar
- 1 tsp chat masala
- 1 tbsp lemon juice

COATING
- ½ cup suji, ¼ cup maida
- ½ tsp salt, ½ tsp pepper

Method

1. Pressure cook cabbage, cauliflower and peas with ½ cup water to give 2 whistles. Reduce heat and keep on low heat for 3-4 minutes. Remove from fire and let the pressure drop. After the pressure drops, mash the vegetables. If there is any extra water present, dry it on fire.
2. Heat oil. Add ginger-garlic paste. Stir. Add pao-bhaji masala. Stir for a minute.
3. Add pressure cooked and mashed vegetables. Saute for 2-3 minutes.
4. Add potatoes and cook, stirring for 3-4 minutes.
5. Add chopped carrots. Add salt, sugar, chat masala and lemon juice. Mix well for 2-3 minutes. Remove from fire and let the mixture cool down. Add fresh bread crumbs. Mix well.
6. Shape into balls. Flatten to get oval, flat tikkis.
7. For the coating, mix suji, maida, salt and pepper and spread on a plate.
8. Roll the tikkis over the maida- suji mixture to coat well. Refrigerate for 2 hours to get crisp nuggets.
9. At serving time, deep fry 1-2 pieces at a time in medium hot oil till crisp. Remove on paper napkins. Sprinkle some chat masala and serve hot.

Quick Paneer Bites

Add taste and texture to paneer triangles by dipping them twice – first in a garlicky batter and then in a dry coating that makes a light crust.

serves 3-4

Ingredients

- 200 gm paneer cut into ¼" thick, triangular pieces,
- sprinkle chat masala on paneer
  BATTER
- 4 tbsp flour (maida)
- 2-3 flakes garlic - crushed
- 1/3 cup water (approx.)
- ½ tsp chilli powder
- ½ tsp chaat masala
- ½ tsp salt to taste
- a pinch carom seeds (ajwain)
  COATING
- 1/3 cup bread crumbs
- 4 tbsp sesame seeds (til)
- 1 tbsp semolina (suji)
- pinch of dry orange red colour
- oil for frying

Method

1. Mix all the ingredients of the batter in a shallow flat bowl.
2. Mix all the coating ingredients in large flat plate, to spread out the mixture.
3. Dip the paneer pieces in the batter. Remove from batter and toss in the coating mixture to coat all sides. Fry the paneer pieces, one at a time, till crisp. Drain on paper napkins to absorb excess oil. Serve hot.

Hidden Veggie Pizza

Children don't want to eat veggies on a pizza. So I have mixed vegetables with the tomato sauce and then spread them on the pizza so that the visibility of veggies gets lessened. They feel they are enjoying their regular cheese pizza.

makes 2

Ingredients

- 2 ready-made pizza bases
  TOMATO SAUCE
- 300 gm (4) tomatoes - blanched (put in hot water for 3-4 minutes and peeled) and chopped finely
- ½ cup readymade tomato puree
- ¼ carrot - grated finely
- ½ cup zucchini - grated finely
- ½ cup grated cauliflower
- 4-5 flakes garlic - crushed
- 1 tsp dried oregano
- salt & freshly ground pepper to taste
- 1 tbsp butter
  TOPPING
- 1 capsicum, tomato, onion - cut into ½" pieces
- ¼ cup corn
- 100 gms mozzarella or pizza cheese - grated
- 1-2 tbsp olive oil

Method

1. For the tomato sauce, heat butter in a pan. Add carrot, zuchini and cauliflower. Cook for 5 minutes till soft. Add garlic. Stir and immediately add tomatoes and all other ingredients of the sauce. Add ½ cup water. Bring to a boil. Lower heat and simmer on low heat for 5 minutes, stirring occasionally until it is reduced in quantity and thick enough to spread without being runny. Remove sauce from fire.

2. Brush pizza base with butter or olive oil on both sides. Spoon some tomato sauce mixture over pizza base, leaving ½" all around the edges.

3. Sprinkle mozzarella cheese. Drizzle some olive oil. Arrange capsicum, tomato, onion and corn. Bake in a preheated oven at 200°C/400°F for 10 minutes until golden and crisp. Serve.

Kandhari Canapes

These unusual potato canapés are baked, then topped with sweet mango chutney and readymade namkeen bhujia!

serves 4

Ingredients

CANAPES
- 1 cup boiled and mashed potatoes
- 4 tbsp cornflour
- ½ tsp salt
- ¼ tsp crushed black pepper
- 1 tsp oil
- 2 tbsp finely chopped parsley or coriander leaves

TOPPING
- 1 tbsp mango chutney to spread
- 2-3 tbsp aloo bhujia
- 3-4 tbsp fresh anaar ke daane
- a few coriander leaves

Method

1. Mix mashed potatoes, cornflour, salt, pepper and oil to make a soft dough.
2. Spread a polythene bag on the kitchen platform. Place the potato dough on it.
3. Roll out to a round chappati, slightly thinner then ¼".
4. Cut it with a design or a round cookie cutter.
5. Grease a baking tray lightly. Place the potato canapes on it.
6. Bake at 180°C for 30 minutes till golden.
7. Brush with melted butter and grill for 3-4 minutes to get brown and crisp. Remove from oven and let them cool. Remove from tray.
8. To serve, spread mango chutney on each canape. Sprinkle some namkeen bhujia and 1 tbsp anar ke daane fresh. Serve topped with coriander leaves.

Chilli Soya Bites

■ Soya nuggets are transformed with a marinade, then lavishly coated with sauce. Little hands will find the elegant presentation on toothpicks a lot of fun!

serves 10-12

Ingredients
- 8 soya nutri nuggets (chunks)
- 1 onion - cut into 8 pieces and separated
- 1 capsicum - cut into ¾" pieces
- 2 tbsp all-in-one stir fry sauce
- a pinch of sugar
- 1 tsp sesame seeds (til)
- a few tooth picks, 1 tsp oil
- 1 tsp crushed or very finely chopped garlic
  MARINADE (MIX TOGETHER)
- 2 tbsp tomato sauce
- 1 tsp soya sauce
- 1 tbsp red chilli sauce
- 1 tsp vinegar
- ½ tsp salt and ¼ tsp white pepper, or to taste

Method
1. Boil 5-6 cups water with 1 tsp salt. Add nuggets and boil for 3-4 minutes or till soft. Remove from water. Squeeze well and keep aside.
2. Marinate the soya chunks, onion & capsicum in the marinade mixture. Keep aside till serving time.
3. Heat a non-stick pan. Reduce flame. Add minced garlic and stir.
4. Add the marinated ingredients and saute for 5 minutes, keeping them in a single layer in the pan.
5. Add all-in-one stir fry sauce and a pinch of sugar. Spread out the veggies in the pan and sprinkle sesame seeds. Remove from pan.
6. Skewer a capsicum piece, soya ball and lastly an onion on the tooth pick. Serve hot.

Meal Time
Dishes

From a child's point of view, 'A Happy Meal' is one in which he loves the look, feel and taste of the food. From a parent's point of view, the food should be packed with the best nutrition required by a growing child. In this chapter you will learn how to make a meal that makes everyone happy!

Mexican Quesadillas

Pronounced as 'keseidiyas," LL being pronounced as "Y". A good melting cheese like mozzarella is important for this snack.

serves 4

Ingredients

CORN TORTILLAS
- ½ cups maize flour (makai ka atta)
- ½ cup flour (maida)
- ½ tsp salt

FILLING
- 150 gm mozzarella cheese - grated (1½ cups)
- 1 tbsp butter
- 1 cup boiled and mashed potatoes
- ¼ tsp chilli flakes
- ¼ tsp mustard
- salt and pepper to taste
- 1 tomato - remove pulp and chop finely
- 1 onion - very finely chopped
- ½ cup frozen corn
- 2 tbsp ready-made salsa

Method

1. Knead makkai ka atta, maida and salt with warm water to make a pliable dough. Roll thin round chappati. Place on a hot tawa. Cook for a minute on medium heat. Turn over and cook the other side for a minute or till brown specks start appearing. Do not make them crisp. Remove from heat.

2. Heat 1 tbsp butter in a pan, add chopped onions and cook for 5 minutes on medium heat till light brown. Add corn. Remove from fire and add mashed potatoes. Add salt, pepper, red chilli flakes and mustard. Add tomato pieces. Stir continuously on flame for 2-3 minutes till properly mixed. Remove from fire. Add cheese to the potato mix.

3. At serving time, spread some potato-cheese mixture on half of the tortilla. Fold over the other half to get a semi circle. Press well so that the edges stick together. Pan fry till golden. Cut into 3 pieces. Serve hot with salsa.

Kathi Nugget Rolls

These rolls are made with paranthas. They are filled with a delicious mixture of soya nuggets, tomatoes and onions. Soya proteins enhance muscle and organ development in children.

serves 4

Ingredients

MARINATE TOGETHER
- 1 cup soya nuggets - soaked in warm water for ½ hour, drained & squeezed, wash in 2-3 changes of water
- 1 tbsp cornflour, ½ tsp salt
- 1½ tsp ginger-garlic paste

PARANTHAS
- 2 cups wheat flour (atta)
- ½ tsp salt, ½ cup milk

FILLING
- 2 onions - cut into 4 pieces and separated
- 2 firm tomatoes - cut into 4 pieces
- 3 tbsp oil,
- salt n pepper to taste
- ½ tsp carom seeds (ajwain)
- ½ tsp soya sauce
- ½ tbsp tomato sauce
- ½ tsp vinegar

Method

1. Marinate the nuggets with cornflour, salt and ginger-garlic paste. Leave aside for 15 minutes.
2. Mix atta with salt and milk with enough water to a smooth dough. Cover and keep aside.
3. Heat 2 tbsp oil in a kadhai. Add the marinated soya nuggets to it and keep stir frying for 5-7 minutes or till slightly brown. Remove from the kadhai.
4. Heat 1 tbsp of oil in the same kadhai, add ajwain and onion. Fry on high flame for 3 minutes. Add tomatoes and fry for 2 minutes. Add the fried soya nuggets, mix well for 2 minutes.
5. Add both the sauces, vinegar, a pinch of salt and a pinch of pepper. Mix for 2 minutes.
6. Make round paranthas with the prepared dough and spread a line of the nugget filling and roll it up. Wrap it in a paper napkin at one end and serve.

Macaroni

All over the world children adore the taste of macaroni and cheese – bake it, serve hot, and watch it disappear!

serves 2

Ingredients

- 50 gm (½ cup) - macaroni
- 2 tsp oil
- 6-7 tbsp cheddar cheese - grated
  SAUCE
- 1 tbsp butter
- 1½ tbsp wheat flour (atta)
- 1 cup milk
- ½ tsp salt or to taste
- a pinch of black pepper powder
- ½ cup corn kernels - frozen or boiled

Method

1. Boil 3-4 cups water with 1 tsp oil and ½ tsp salt. Add macaroni and boil for 7-8 minutes or until it turns soft.
2. Strain. Apply 1 tsp oil over the macaroni and keep aside.
3. To prepare the sauce, heat butter in a pan. Add flour and stir on low heat for 2-3 minutes.
4. Remove from fire. Add milk, stirring continuously. Return to fire. Cook for 2-3 minutes or until sauce thickens.
5. Add corn, salt and pepper. Stir. Remove from fire.
6. Put half of the grated cheese in it and mix well.
7. Pre-heat oven to 180°C/350°F.
8. Spread little sauce in an oven proof dish. Put macaroni. Pour the remaining sauce on top to cover the macaroni.
9. Sprinkle grated cheese and 1 tsp corn on top.
10. Bake at 180°C for 8-9 minutes. Drizzle some ketchup. Serve hot.

Penne with Veggies

This recipe gives two options for the cheesy cream sauce – leave it white or stir in tomato puree for a change of colour and flavour.

serves 2

Ingredients

- 1 cup whole wheat pasta or any other pasta of your choice
- 2 tbsp oil
- ½ cup chopped mixed vegetables (cauliflower, carrot, capsicum, zucchini, beans or peas)
- 1 onion - chopped
- 1 tsp garlic paste (5-6 flakes of garlic - crushed to a paste)
- 4 tbsp ready-made tomato puree
- 2 tsp sugar
- salt and pepper to taste
  CREAMY MIXTURE
- ¼ cup thick cream
- 2 tbsp cheese spread
- 3 tbsp milk

Method

1. Boil 6 cups water with 1 tsp oil and 1 tsp salt. Add pasta to boiling water. Boil for 8-10 minutes till pasta turns soft. Remove from fire. Drain the water. Sprinkle 1 tsp olive oil on the paste and keep aside.
2. Heat oil in a frying pan, add garlic and onions and cook for ½ minute.
3. Add cauliflower, zucchini/peas, beans & carrot. Cook for 4-5 min. or till vegetables are tender.
4. Add capsicum and pasta. Cook for ½ minute.
5. Add tomato puree and sugar. Cook for a minute. Keep aside till serving time.
6. At serving time, mix cream, cheese spread and milk together in a bowl. Stir into the pasta, cook for about 2 minutes. The cream sauce would thicken and coat the pasta. Check salt. Serve hot with garlic bread.

Note

If you want the pasta to have a white saucy look then omit the tomato puree and sugar.

Multigrain Wraps

■ Make a pancake batter using suji, besan and oats. Use paneer in the filling for extra nutrition points.

makes 6

Ingredients

WRAPS
- ½ cup sooji
- ½ cup besan
- ½ cup oats
- 2 tbsp coriander leaves
- ½ tsp garam masala
- ¼ tsp amchoor
- 1 tsp roasted jeera powder
- 1 tsp black salt, ¼ tsp salt
- 2 cups water, approx.

FILLING
- 1 tbsp oil
- ½ tsp cumin seeds (jeera)
- 1 onion - chopped
- 1 tsp grated ginger
- ¾ tsp salt, ¼ tsp pepper
- 50 gm paneer or 1 boiled potato - cut into ¼" cubes
- ½ cup boiled/frozen corn or peas
- ½ cup grated carrot
- a pinch of sugar
- 1 tsp lemon juice
- 1 tbsp each of coriander & mint leaves
- 1 tomato - chopped

TO SPREAD
- 6 tsp tomato ketchup

Method

1. Mix all ingredients of the wraps. Add enough water gradually to make a pouring pancake batter of coating consistency. Keep aside for 5-10 minuters. Whisk the batter for a minute till smooth.

2. For the filling, heat 1 tbsp oil. Add jeera. Wait for a minute. Add chopped onions and grated ginger. Saute onion till soft. Add carrots and stir for 2-3 minutes. Add boiled potato/paneer and stir for a minute.

3. Add corn/peas, salt and pepper. Stir.

4. Add mint and coriander. Stir for a minute. Add tomato. Add lemon juice and a pinch of sugar. Mix. Keep filling aside.

5. To make a pancake, grease a non stick tawa and heat on fire. Remove pan from fire. Pour one kadchhi of batter and spread lightly to a roti size. Return to low heat. Drizzle 1 tsp oil from the sides immediately. Cook for 2-3 minutes till edges turn golden. Turn side and cook the other side on high heat.

6. Reduce heat. Spread tomato ketchup on the pancake. Put some filling and fold like a dosa. Remove from tawa and serve hot.

Kids Popeye Semolina Burgers

A brand new innovation – burger patties made with semolina, spinach and besan.

serves 4

Ingredients
- 4 dinner rolls or 4 burger buns
- 4 tbsp ready-made mango chutney or tomato ketchup
- 4 tbsp ready-made mayonnaise (optional)

PATTY
- 4 tbsp butter or oil
- 1 onion - thinly sliced
- 1 tsp grated ginger
- 1 tsp grated garlic
- 20 spinach (palak) leaves or 20 leaves of baby bok choy
- ½ cup semolina (suji) - dry roast in a kadhai till fragrant
- 1 tsp salt
- ¼ tsp red chilli powder
- 1½ tsp dark soya sauce
- ½ cup gram flour (besan) - dry roast in a kadhai till fragrant

TOPPING
- ¾ cup grated carrot
- 1 tsp grated ginger
- 5 tsp vinegar or lemon juice
- 1½ tsp mild tabasco sauce
- 1 tsp powdered sugar

Method

1. Mix carrot, ginger, vinegar, tabasco and sugar in a bowl. Keep aside.
2. Heat 2 tbsp butter or oil in a wok or frying pan. Add onion and cook over medium heat for 1 minute. Add ginger and garlic, cook for a minute. Add spinach and semolina, stir fry for 2 minutes. Add salt, red chilli powder, soy sauce and mix well. Cook for 1 minute. Add ½ cup water, cook till absolutely dry for about 2 minutes.
3. Add roasted gram flour. Mix well. Remove. Cool slightly.
4. Make ½" thin 4 big flat patties with the mixture. Keep aside till serving time.
5. Heat oil in a kadhai. Deep fry 1 patty at a time in hot oil till golden brown on both sides. Repeat with remaining patties. Drain on paper napkins.
6. Halve rolls or buns horizontally. Lightly butter if desired and toast on a pan till crisp on both the sides or grill for 3-4 minutes in a hot oven till crisp.
7. Place lower halves of the buns on individual serving plates. On each piece spread mango chutney. Place a hot patty on it and top it with carrot mixture. Spoon some mayonnaise (optional). Cover with the top half of the roll or bun. Serve hot with ketchup and onion rings.

Vegetable & Cheese Paranthas

■ These paranthas have a secret ingredient – almond powder in the dough.

makes 6

Ingredients

DOUGH
- 2 cups wheat flour (atta)
- 1 tbsp badam - powdered, see page 8
- 1 tsp salt
- ½ tsp turmeric (haldi)
- 1 tbsp oil or ghee
- ¾ cup water for kneading, approx.
- 6 tbsp ghee for frying

STUFFING
- ½ cup grated cheddar cheese
- 4 tbsp grated carrot (gajar)
- 4 tbsp grated cauliflower (gobhi)
- 4 tbsp boiled & mashed peas
- 2 tbsp finely chopped coriander
- ½ tsp salt
- ½ tsp pepper, ½ tsp oregano

Method

1. Mix atta, badam powder, salt, haldi and 1 tbsp ghee in a bowl (paraat). Gradually add water and knead to a soft, smooth dough. Cover with a damp cloth and keep aside for 30 minutes.
2. Mix all the ingredients of the stuffing in a bowl.
3. Make 12 marble sized balls of the dough. Roll out a ball into a very thin round (chappati).
4. On the roti, put 3 tbsp of the filling, leaving ½" from all around.
5. Roll out another ball to a round roti of the same size. Place this on the roti with the stuffing. Press well to stick the rotis together. Gently roll out with a rolling pin (belan).
6. Cook parantha on a hot tawa. When the underside is cooked, turn to cook the other side. Smear some ghee or oil or butter to serve.

Protein Pulao

■ This can be a one-dish meal which can be so convenient on a too-busy day.

serves 3

Ingredients
- 1 cup rice
- 2 tbsp lobhia - soaked in some water
- 2 tbsp red kidney beans (rajma) - soaked in some water
- 1 small carrot - cut into 1" round slices
- 2 large onions - chopped
- 2 medium size tomatoes - chopped
- 1½ tsp salt, 4 tbsp oil

GRIND TO PASTE
- ½ " piece of ginger
- 1 flake of garlic
- ¾ cup chopped coriander leaves
- 2 cloves (laung)
- 2 green cardamoms (chhoti elaichi)
- ½" stick cinnamon (dalchini)
- 1 tsp black cumin (shah jeera) or ½ tsp regular cumin (jeera)
- ½ tsp turmeric (haldi)

Method
1. Soak rajma and lobhia in separate bowls for 4 hours or overnight.
2. Wash rice and drain.
3. In a cooker heat oil and add onion. Stir fry on medium heat till golden.
4. Add tomatoes, prepared paste and haldi. Stir well for 2-3 minutes.
5. Add rice, soaked pulses, carrot and salt.
6. Add 2¼ cup water. Mix well. Pressure cook for 7 minutes. Remove from fire. Let the pressure drop by itself.
7. Serve hot with any kind of raita.

Healthy Mixed Dal

A hearty tomato-based masala is cooked with care then added to a classic mix of dals that are simmered together.

makes 6

Ingredients
- ¼ cup split bengal gram (channa dal)
- ¼ cup red kidney beans (rajma)
- ½ cup black beans (sabut urad dal)
- 2 medium size onions
- 1 tbsp chopped garlic
- 3 medium tomatoes - chopped
- ¼ cup chopped coriander leaves (hara dhania)
- 5-6 tbsp oil
- ½ tbsp cumin (jeera) powder
- 1 tbsp dry fenugreek leaves (kasuri methi) - roasted in a kadhai for 1-2 minutes
- 3 tbsp butter, 1 tsp salt

Method
1. Clean, wash and soak black beans, bengal gram and red kidney beans in sufficient water for at least 6 hours.
2. Drain soaked dals. Add 4 cups of water and pressure cook on high heat in a cooker till 4 whistles and then cook on slow fire for 30 minutes. Keep aside.
3. Heat oil in a pan and add chopped onion. Stir fry till golden brown.
4. Add garlic and stir fry for 10-15 minutes.
5. Add cumin powder and cook for a minute.
6. Add tomatoes and stir fry on high flame for 3-4 minutes or till masala leaves oil.
7. Add salt, remove from fire.
8. Add this masala to the dal. Crush roasted dry fenugreek leaves between the palms, sprinkle on the dal in the pressure cooker and cook for 5 minutes.
9. Add butter and coriander. Remove to a serving bowl.

Lauki and Tomato Soup

A delicious light summer soup!

makes 4

Ingredients
- ½ kg tomatoes - roughly chopped
- 250 gms (1 small) lauki or ghiya (bottle gourd) - peeled and chopped
- ½" piece ginger, 6-8 saboot kali mirch (peppercorns)
- 1 onion - chopped
- 1 tbsp butter
- ¾ tsp salt, ½ tsp pepper or to taste
- a pinch of sugar, 1 tsp tomato ketchup, optional
- fresh coriander to garnish

Method
1. In a pressure cooker, boil the tomatoes, ghiya, ginger, saboot kali mirch and onion with 4 cups of water to give 1 whistle. Keep on low flame for 4-5 minutes. Remove from fire.
2. Cool and puree in a blender. Strain the puree. Boil soup. Add butter, ketchup, salt, pepper and sugar. Add fresh coriander.
3. Simmer for a few minutes. Serve hot.

Note

For variation, instead of ghiya one may use 2 tbsp of moong dhuli dal and juice of half a lemon. Try topping the soup with 1 tsp of butter, for those who do not mind a little fat!

Karaari Arbi

■ A new taste, a touch of ajwain, and a tight crispness – ingredients for addiction!

serves 4

Ingredients
- ½ kg colocassia (arbi)
- 5 tbsp oil
- 1 tsp carom seeds (ajwain)
- 1 tsp turmeric (haldi) powder
- 1¼ tsp coriander (dhania) powder
- ¼ tsp garam masala
- 1 tsp salt

Method
1. Wash and peel colocassia. Cut each lengthwise into 2 pieces. Cut each piece into thin fingers.
2. Heat 5 tbsp oil in a big kadhai or a pan. Add carom seeds and wait for 1 minute.
3. Add colocassia fingers, turmeric, coriander powder, garam masala & salt. Mix well for 2-3 minutes.
4. Cook covered on low heat for 8-10 minutes, keeping them separated from each other.
5. Cook uncovered on high heat for 8-10 minutes or till crisp. Serve hot.

> **Note**
> You can microwave the arbi with ½ cup water, covered for 8 min. Peel and cut the boiled arbi into 4 pieces lengthwise. Heat oil with ajwain and spices. Add arbi and stir fry for 5 minutes. Serve.

Pav Bhaji

■ Use a microwave to cook this potato and vegetable mixture that is soft but not mushy. Butter adds that yummy touch of luxury!

serves 4

Ingredients

- 3 onions - chopped finely
- 3 potatoes
- 2 carrots - peeled and chopped
- ½ cup peas
- 1½ cups chopped cauliflower
- 1 cup chopped cabbage
- 3 tbsp oil
- 3 tbsp butter
- 2 tsp ginger-garlic paste
- 2½ tbsp pav bhaji masala
- ¼ tsp turmeric powder (haldi)
- 1½ tsp salt
- 3 tomatoes - chopped
- 1 tbsp chopped coriander

Method

1. Wash potatoes. Put in a plastic bag and microwave for 5 minutes. Peel and mash coarsely.
2. In a deep microproof bowl, put carrots, peas, cauliflower and cabbage. Add ½ cup water. Mix and microwave for 8 minutes. Let it cool. Blend roughly in a mixer for 1-2 seconds. Do not make it into a paste.
3. In a microproof dish add oil, onions, ginger-garlic paste, 2 tbsp pav bhaji masala and haldi. Mix well. Microwave for 6 minutes.
4. Add tomatoes and the roughly mashed vegetables. Mix well. Add 2 tbsp butter, 1½ tsp salt. Cover and microwave for 10 minutes. Stir once in between.
5. Add 1 cup water. Mix and microwave for 5 minutes.
6. Add 1 tsp pav bhaji masala, 2 tbsp chopped coriander and 1 tbsp butter. Mix and serve.

Pasta in Quick Tomato Sauce

- Enjoy the eye-appeal given by strips of red and green tomato and capsicum, tossed along with the pasta in a creamy tomato sauce.

serves 4

Ingredients

- 3 cups penne or any other pasta
- 1 medium capsicum - chopped finely
- 1 + 3 tbsp olive oil
- 2 tsp crushed garlic
- 1 cup ready-made tomato puree
- ¾ tsp pepper, 1 tsp oregano
- 1 tsp salt, ½ cup milk
- ½ cup cream (optional)
- ½ cup grated cheese

Method

1. Boil 8-10 cups of water in a large pan. Add 2 tsp salt and 1 tbsp of any cooking oil. Drop pasta in boiling water. Boil for 8-10 minutes or till pasta turns soft but is still firm. Remove from fire and let the pasta stay in hot water for 2-3 minutes. Strain, reserving 1 cup pasta water. Sprinkle 1-2 tbsp olive oil on the pasta and toss well. Keep aside.
2. Heat 1 tbsp olive oil in a wok, add ½ tsp garlic, saute for ½ minute. Add capsicum and stir for 2 minutes. Add boiled pasta, saute for 1-2 minutes. Add ¼ tsp pepper and ½ tsp oregano. Toss, remove pasta from the wok.
3. In the same wok heat 3 tbsp olive oil. Add 1½ tsp crushed garlic. Stir till it changes colour.
4. Add 1 cup ready-made tomato puree. Cook for 3-4 minutes or till oil separates.
5. Add ½ tsp pepper, ½ tsp oregano and 1 tsp salt. Mix. Reduce heat and cook for 2 minutes. Add boiled pasta with capsicum, toss well. Keep aside.
6. At serving time, heat the pasta on fire. Add cheese, milk and cream. Toss well. Check salt and pepper. If the pasta appears thick, thin it down with pasta water. Remove from fire. Serve hot with garlic bread.

TIP

For fresh tomato puree: Tomatoes are roughly chopped and ground to a puree in a mixer-grinder. Instead of using raw tomatoes they are sometimes blanched before pureeing. If you have any other pasta shape at home e.g macaroni, rigatoni etc., use it instead of penne.

Instant Idli

These idlis are ready in about 30 minutes – overnight soaking, the old-fashioned way, is not required.

serves 8

Ingredients

- 1 cup suji (rava), coarse semolina,
- 1½ tbsp oil
- 1 cup curd (dahi)
- a few curry leaves or a few cashewnuts
- ½ tsp soda-bi-carb (mitha soda)
- ¾ tsp salt
- ½ cup water, approx.

Method

1. Heat 1½ tbsp oil in a kadhai. Add suji and mix well. Stir on low heat for 2 minutes till it just starts to change colour. Remove from fire. Add salt. Mix well. Let it cool.

2. Add curd to the suji (suji should cool down) mixture. Mix well with a spoon or a wire whisk. Add soda-bi-carb. Mix very well till smooth. Add water and mix well again to get a thickish batter, but it should not be too thick. It should fall easily when dropped from a spoon. Keep the batter aside for 10 minutes. Take an idli mould and put 1-2 drops of oil in each round cup and spread it evenly with your fingers. Put a split cashewnut or curry leaf in each cup. Top with some batter.

3. Put a big deep pan filled with 1" high water on fire, to boil. After the water boils, reduce heat. Place the idli mould into the pan of water. Increase heat to medium. Cover the pan with a lid. Steam for 14 minutes undisturbed on medium flame. Insert a knife in the idli, if it comes out clean it's done. Remove from fire. Remove idlis from the mould after 5 minutes with the help of a knife. Leave them covered in the stand in the pan till serving time.

4. To serve, steam them again for 3-4 minutes till heated properly. Serve hot with coconut chutney.

Paneer Makhani

Cream and cashew nut paste add a luscious touch to a classic favourite.

serves 4

Ingredients

- 250 gm paneer - cut into 1" cubes
- 5 large (500 gm) tomatoes - each cut into 4 pieces
- 2 tbsp butter and 2 tbsp oil
- 4-5 flakes garlic & 1" piece ginger - ground to a paste (1½ tsp ginger-garlic paste)
- 1 tbsp dry fenugreek leaves (kasoori methi)
- 1 tsp tomato ketchup
- 2 tsp dhania powder
- ½ tsp garam masala
- 1 tsp salt, or to taste
- ½ tsp red chilli powder, preferably degi mirch
- ½ cup water
- ½-1 cup milk, approx.
- ½ cup cream (optional)
- 3 tbsp cashewnuts (kaju) - soak in hot water for 20 minutes, drain and grind to a smooth paste with a little water

Method

1. Boil tomatoes in ½ cup water. Simmer for 4-5 minutes on low heat till tomatoes turn soft. Remove from heat and cool. Grind the tomatoes along with the water to a smooth puree.
2. Heat oil and butter in a kadhai. Add ginger-garlic paste. Mix.
3. When paste starts to change colour add the above tomato puree and cook till dry. Add dry fenugreek leaves & tomato ketchup.
4. Add masalas - coriander powder, garam masala, salt and red chilli powder. Mix well for a few seconds. Cook till oil separates.
5. Add cashew paste. Mix well for 2 minutes. Add water. Boil. Simmer on low heat for 4-5 minutes. Reduce heat.
6. Add the paneer cubes. Remove from heat. Keep aside to cool for about 5 minutes.
7. Add enough milk to the cold paneer masala to get a thick curry, mix gently. (Remember to add milk only after the masala is no longer hot, to prevent the milk from curdling. After adding milk, heat curry on low heat.)
8. Heat on low heat, stirring continuously till just about to boil.
9. Add cream, keeping the heat very low and stirring continuously. Remove from heat immediately and transfer to a serving dish. Swirl 1 tbsp cream over the hot paneer in the dish. Serve immediately.

VARIATION

For dakshini tadka, heat 1 tbsp oil. Add ½ tsp rai. After 30 seconds add 4-5 curry leaves. Stir. Remove from heat. Add a pinch of red chilli powder and pour over the hot paneer makhani in the dish.

Sambar

A miraculous transformation of the humble arhar dal, with tangy, sweet and spicy tones.

makes 6

Ingredients

- 1 cup red gram dal (tuvar dal)
- ½ tsp turmeric powder
- 1 lemon sized ball of tamarind
- 3 tbsp oil
- 1 tsp mustard seeds
- 2 sprigs curry leaves
- 3-4 green chillies, slit
- 1 cup peeled Madras onions (the small red variety) or 1 onion cut into ¾" pieces
- 1 small carrot - cut into slices
- 6-8 french beans - cut into 1" pieces
- 2 tbsp sambar powder
- salt to taste
- a pinch of jaggery (gur)

Method

1. Cook dal with ½ tsp turmeric powder in a pressure cooker.
2. Boil the tamarind in boiling water and squeeze to extract the pulp.
3. Heat oil and add the mustard. When done, add the curry leaves, green chillies, onion and fry until the onions are soft and brown.
4. Add carrot and beans. Saute for 2 minutes.
5. Add the tamarind extract and cook for 5 minutes till tamarind dries up.
6. Dissolve the sambar masala in ¼ cup water to make a paste. Add to the vegetables and stir for 1-2 minutes till fragrant.
7. Now add the dal, salt and some water to thin down the mixture if the mixture is thick. Cook for 10 minutes. Add jaggery. Simmer for a few minutes.

Vada

- If the vada mixture becomes loose and is difficult to handle, add 2-3 tbsp besan (gram flour) to the daal paste.

serves 4-5

Ingredients

- 1 cup split black gram dal (dhuli urad dal)
- ¼ tsp asafoetida (hing) powder
- 3 green chillies - finely chopped
- 1 tsp pepper corns (saboot kali mirch) - crushed
- 10-15 curry leaves - chopped
- 1½ tsp salt or to taste
- 2 pinches baking powder, oil for frying

Method

1. Soak the dal for 2 hours only. Do not soak for a longer period. Drain & grind dal along with hing to a thick, rough paste using very little water. Do not make it too smooth.
2. Mix green chillies, crushed pepper corns, curry leaves, salt and baking powder. Beat well (vigorously) for 2-3 minutes, with the fingers till dal turns fluffy. Do not keep the paste aside but fry vadas immediately If the salted paste is fried after keeping in the fridge for a few hours, the vadas turn out very oily.
3. Heat oil in a kadhai. Wet the back of a big katori or a flat bottomed bowl. Put a ball of the paste on it. Flatten it a little. Dip a finger in water and make a big hole in the centre of the vada.
4. Then slip the vada gently in oil. Do not touch the vada till the bottom gets a little cooked. Now turn gently, with a knife, to cook the other side. Fry 4-5 vadas together on medium flame till golden brown.
5. Serve hot with sambhar.

NOTE

The dal should not be soaked for too long, because on doing so, the vadas absorb too much oil on frying. You may grind the dal and keep it in the fridge overnight without adding anything to it. Do not grind the dal too much. It should be a rough, thick paste. Chopped onions may be added to the dal paste at the time of frying. Do not add earlier as onions leave water and make the paste loose.

Chilli Paneer Dosa

This recipe makes a perfect dosa every time. Give a Chinese-flavoured paneer filling for fantastic Fusion Food!

makes 10

Ingredients

DOSA
- ¾ cup parboiled rice (sela or ushna chaawal)
- ¾ cups ordinary quality rice (permal chaawal)
- ½ cup dehusked black gram (dhuli urad dal)
- 1 tsp fenugreek seeds (methi dana)

CHILLI PANEER
- 250 gm paneer - cut into 1" cubes
- 1 capsicum - chopped finely
- 1½ tsp soya sauce
- 1½ tsp vinegar
- ¾ tsp salt, ¾ tsp pepper
- 2 tbsp tomato sauce
- 1 tsp garlic - crushed
- 2 tbsp plain flour (maida)

Method

1. Soak both rice, dal and fenugreek seeds together in a pan for at least 6 hours.
2. Grind together finely to a paste, using some of the water in which it was soaked.
3. Add more water to the paste, if required, to get a batter of medium pouring consistency. Mix well. Keep aside for 12 hours or overnight in a warm place, to get fermented. In winter, wrap the batter in a thick towel or a warm shawl. After fermentation, the batter should rise a little and smell sour.
4. Mix paneer with soya sauce, vinegar, salt, pepper, tomato sauce and crushed garlic. Keep aside to marinate for 15 minutes.
5. Sprinkle some maida on the paneer. Mix gently to coat. Deep fry till golden.
6. Crush the fried paneer with fingers roughly. Add capsicum. Check salt.
7. For dosas, add salt to the batter and mix nicely with a kadchi, before preparing dosas.
8. Heat a non stick tawa on medium heat. Pour a tsp oil on the tawa. Sprinkle a pinch of salt on the oil. Rub the tawa with piece of onion or potato.
9. Remove tawa from heat & pour 1 heaped kadchi of batter. Spread quickly. Return to heat. Cook the dosa a little. Pour 2 tsp of oil on the dosa and the sides. Cover for 1-2 minutes.
10. After it turns golden brown, gently loosen the sides and bottom.
11. Put 3 tbsp of the filling in the centre of the dosa in a row and spread a little.
12. Fold over from both sides. Remove from tawa. Serve hot with coconut chutney.

Sandwiches

An 18th century English aristocrat, the Earl of Sandwich, ordered his servant to bring him meat tucked between 2 pieces of bread so that he could continue playing cards without getting them greasy - and so the 'sandwich' was born! Over the decades it gained rapidly in popularity among busy people with busy lives.

Veg. Club Sandwiches

■ Toasted buttered bread supports this classic, three-layered construction. A special, zesty mayonnaise joins the flavours of cucumber and cheese to satisfy the craving of every hungry child.

serves 2-3

Ingredients

- 50 gms paneer - cut into thin slices
- 2 cheese slices
- 6 slices of brown bread
- some butter - enough to spread
- 1 small cucumber (kheera) - wash & slice along with the peel into paper-thin slices

MIX TOGETHER IN A BOWL

- 4 tbsp mayonnaise
- $\frac{1}{4}$ cup finely chopped capsicum (simla mirch)
- $\frac{1}{4}$ cup finely shredded cabbage (band gobhi)
- $\frac{1}{4}$ cup grated carrot (gajar)
- $\frac{1}{4}$ tsp pepper
- $\frac{1}{2}$ tsp mustard paste

Method

1. Mix mayonnaise, capsicum, cabbage, carrot, pepper and mustard paste in a bowl. Mix well. Check seasonings. Add more if required.
2. Slice paneer into thin slices and sprinkle salt and pepper on it.
3. Toast all the bread slices and spread some butter on one side of each toast. Place a cheese slice. Lay some cucumber slices on the cheese. Place another buttered toast on it, with the butter side down on the cucumber pieces.
4. Place a paneer slice on the bread. Spread some mayonnaise mixture on the last slice of bread and press on the paneer slice. Keep this sandwich aside.
5. Repeat with the other slices to make another sandwich.
6. Trim the edges of a sandwich and cut each sandwich diagonally into four pieces. Serve sandwich with french fries and tomato ketchup.
7. To decorate the sandwich, pierce a small piece of lettuce or cabbage leaf through a tooth pick and top with a cherry, grape or olive.

VARIATION

You can use a thin vegetable cutlet instead of the paneer slices as a variation.

Peanut Butter Sandwiches

Toasted bread covered with homemade peanut butter and filled with a crunchy mix of sprouts and onions – an unforgettable experience!

makes 2

Ingredients

- 4 slices of brown bread - toasted in a toaster
- Peanut Butter (Makes ½ cup)
- ¾ cup unsalted roasted peanuts
- 1 tbsp oil
- ¼ slice brown bread
  FILLING
- ½ cup moong sprouts - boiled
  (use ready-made or make at home)
- 1 onion - chopped
- 1 tbsp tomato ketchup
- a pinch of salt, pepper and sugar

Method

1. Put peanuts, oil and bread in a food processor. Process the mixture until it is very smooth.
2. Store your smooth peanut butter in a sealed container in the fridge. It will be good for 2 weeks.
3. Mix boiled sprouts with onion, tomato ketchup, a pinch of salt, pepper and sugar.
4. Spread peanut butter on all the 4 slices of toasted breads. Spread a layer of the filling on top of 2 bread slices. Press the remaining two slices on it. Cut each into 4 square or triangular pieces. Serve.

Tikka Paneer Sandwiches

Make a filling that tastes exactly like everyone's favourite paneer tikka. Toast the sandwich in a pan with a little oil to get melt-in-the-mouth satisfaction.

serves 4

Ingredients

- 200 gm paneer - cut into small pieces
- 1 small capsicum - chopped
- 4 slices of bread - lightly buttered
- 2-3 lettuce leaves - shredded, optional

MARINADE
- ½ cup curd (dahi) - hang in a muslin cloth for 15 minutes
- ½ tsp roasted cumin (bhuna jeera) powder
- ½ tsp red chilli powder
- ½ tsp chaat masala
- ½ tsp salt, or to taste
- ½ tsp haldi
- ½ tsp garam masala
- ½ tsp dhania powder
- 1 tsp ginger garlic paste (8-10 flakes of garlic and 1" piece of ginger - crushed)

Method

1. Mix all ingredients of marinade. Add paneer and capsicum. Keep aside for 15 minutes.

2. Heat 1 tbsp oil in a pan, add marinated paneer and capsicum. Cook on low heat for 5-6 minutes till dry and golden brown from some sides. Sprinkle ¼ tsp each of bhuna jeera, salt, garam masala and dhania powder. Mix. Remove from fire.

3. On each lightly buttered bread, spread some paneer tikka mixture. Sprinkle some shredded lettuce. Cover with another slice. Press gently. Toast in a pan in 1 tsp oil till golden brown from both sides. Cut into two triangles.

Apple & Carrot Sandwiches

Easy to make, pretty to look at, the right size for small fingers, cheesy and crunchy – this one is a winner!

serves 3

Ingredients

- 6 breads slices
  APPLE SPREAD (MIX TOGETHER)
- 1 apple - grated
- 2 tbsp cheese spread
- ¼ tsp salt, ¼ tsp pepper
  CARROT SPREAD
- ¾ cup grated carrot
- 2 tbsp cheese spread
- ¼ tsp salt
- ¼ tsp pepper
- 2 tbsp raisin (kishmish) - chopped

Method

1. Mix all ingredients of the apple and carrot spread separately.
2. Apply the apple spread on one bread slice. Cover with another slice of bread.
3. Spread a layer of the carrot spread on the second slice. Cover with the third slice of bread.
4. Repeat to make more sandwiches. Cut into fingers.

Cheese-Raisin Sandwiches

Salt and sweet combine in a way that is sure to appeal to children.

serves 4

Ingredients

- 8 slices bread, preferably brown - lightly buttered
- 4 tbsp raisins (kishmish) - soak in warm water
- 3 cubes (75 gm) cheese - grated
- 3 tbsp milk, 3 tbsp mayonnaise

Method

1. Strain the raisins soaked in water.
2. Blend the grated cheese with milk and mayonnaise.
3. Add raisins.
4. Butter all the slices lightly. Spread some filling on a slice and cover with another slice. Cut into two and serve.

NOTE
You may reduce the amount of raisins (kishmish) for adults.

Green Peas Sandwiches

Mayonnaise, cheese and crushed green peas are spread on toast then topped with slices of tomato and red capsicum to make a gourmet sandwich!

serves 4

Ingredients

- 8 bread slices
- some butter to spread
- 1 large tomato or
- 1 red capsicum - thinly sliced
  FILLING (MIX TOGETHER)
- 1 cup green peas (matar) - boiled and roughly crushed
- 1 tbsp finely chopped coriander or mixed nuts
- 2 tbsp mayonnaise
- 1 tbsp cheese spread
- ¼ tsp salt, ½ tsp pepper

Method

1. Mix all ingredients of the filling in a bowl. Check salt. Divide into 4 portions.
2. Toast all the bread slices. Apply butter on all slices.
3. Spread 1 portion of the filling over a slice. Arrange the tomato or capsicum slices over the filling.
4. Cover with another slice of toasted bread to make a sandwich. Cut into half, diagonally.
5. Repeat with remaining bread slices, tomato slices and the filling to make three more sandwiches. Serve hot.

Spinach & Corn Sandwiches

■ Cheesy sautéed spinach and corn in the first layer; tomato slices in the second layer – this construction is designed to please everyone.

makes 4 sandwiches

Ingredients

CORN LAYER
- 1½ cups spinach
- 1 tbsp butter
- ½ onion - finely chopped
- 1 tsp chopped garlic
- 3 tbsp cream, 2 tbsp corn
- salt, pepper to taste
- 3-4 tbsp grated cheddar cheese

OTHER INGREDIENTS
- 6 slices of any healthy bread
BUTTER TO SPREAD
- chilli sauce\hot & sweet sauce
- 1 tomato - cut into thin slices
- salt, pepper to taste

Method

1. Microwave spinach with ¾ cup water, ½ tsp salt and ½ tsp sugar for 3 minutes. Drain water and keep in the strainer.
2. Heat 1 tbsp butter. Add onion and garlic. Saute till soft. Add spinach and saute for 2 minutes. Remove from fire.
3. Add cream and corn. Add cheese. Add salt and pepper to taste. Keep corn-spinach aside.
4. Butter a bread slice. Spread half of the corn-spinach mixture. Cover with another slice. Spread chilli sauce on it. Arrange tomato slices and sprinkle some salt-pepper on it. Butter another slice and invert on the tomatoes. Press well and cut into 2 pieces to serve.

Brown Veg. Sandwiches

■ Grate the veggies and cheese to create an interesting texture between the slices of buttered brown bread.

serves 2

Ingredients

- 2 tbsp ready-made mayonnaise or softened butter
- 4 brown bread slices - crust removed
- 4 tbsp finely shredded cabbage or lettuce
- 4 tbsp grated carrot
- 1 cube (25 gm) cheese, grated

Method

1. Spread mayonnaise or softened butter on all 4 slices of brown bread.
2. Sprinkle some cabbage on a slice spread with mayonnaise. Now sprinkle a layer of grated carrots on the cabbage.
3. Grate some cheese over it.
4. Cover with another slice spread generously with mayonnaise or butter.
5. Press well. Cut diagonally into 4 pieces. Make the second sandwich in the same way.
6. Arrange in a serving plate. Serve.

Vegetable Sandwiches

Fresh raw veggies are paired with cheese and mayonnaise to make this hearty sandwich.

serves 2

Ingredients
- 4 slices bread
  FILLING
- 1 cup boiled and mashed potatoes
- 4 tbsp mayonnaise
- 1 tbsp tomato ketchup
- 4 tbsp grated cabbage
- 4 tbsp finely grated carrot
- 2 tbsp chopped green coriander leaves
- 2 tbsp grated cheedar cheese

Method
1. Mix all ingredients of filling in a bowl, adding just enough mayonnaise to get a good spreading consistency. Check seasoning and add salt to taste.
2. Spread half mixture on a plain slice. Place the other slice on it. Press lightly.
3. Serve plain as it is or grill in the oven till crisp and golden brown. Cut into 2 pieces and serve with tomato ketchup.

Croquette Subwich

These bolster-shaped potato croquettes are delicious to eat by themselves. Place them inside French bread which looks a bit like a submarine - and call it a subwich!

serves 2-3

Ingredients

- 1 loaf french bread (9")
- 1 small onion - sliced
- ½ cup shredded lettuce or cabbage

CROQUETTE (POTATO ROLL)

- 1 small onion - finely chopped
- 2 tbsp butter
- 2 small carrots - grated (1 cup)
- 1 cup grated cauliflower
- 2 potatoes - boiled & grated
- 2 tsp cornflour, ¼ tsp pepper
- 1 tbsp tomato ketchup
- 1 tsp salt or to taste

COATING

- 2 tbsp cornflour mixed with ¼ cup water, ½ cup dry maida (flour)
- ¼ cup grated cabbage
- 2½ tbsp ready-made mayonnaise
- 2 tsp milk, ¼ tsp lemon juice
- a pinch of salt and pepper

Method

1. For the croquettes, heat butter in a pan. Add onion. Cook for 2-3 minutes.
2. Add carrots and cauliflower, cook for 4-5 minutes. Mix boiled potatoes. Add cornflour, tomato ketchup, salt and pepper. Mix well and cook for 6-7 minutes. Remove from fire. Shape into long rolls, about 2½" in length.
3. To coat, dip the rolls in a thin cornflour batter and immediately roll over dry flour spread in a plate. Keep aside in the refrigerator to set.
4. Shallow fry croquettes in oil in a pan till crisp.
5. Make a slit in the French loaf going till the end, but let the end be intact. Cut it into 3 pieces. Spread lettuce and onion on each piece. Arrange 2 croquettes on it.
6. Spread the mayonnaise mixture on the croquettes. Sprinkle salt & pepper. Press the top part of bread.
7. Heat 1 tbsp oil in a pan and put the sub in a pan and cook till crisp from both sides. Serve hot.

Sweet Delights

The sweeter side of food makes the child feel happy. And feeling happy motivates good health. Childhood is a time of joy, and every day is a celebration in which desserts have place of pride.

Spinach & Beetroot Cookies

■ Kids will be curious to try something new – cookies that are coloured red and green instead of beige or brown.

makes 30

Ingredients

- 100 gms butter - salted
- 50 gms powdered sugar (¼ cup + 1 tbsp)
- 100 gms maida (1 cup)
- 2 tbsp raw spinach puree or 2 tbsp raw beetroot puree

Method

1. Cream butter + sugar until very light and fluffy with an electric beater.
2. Add spinach / beetroot puree to the above mixture and beat well.
3. Add maida gradually to the mixture and mix well to get a soft dough consistency.
4. Line a cookie sheet with brown paper. Grease the sheet. Fill the cookie mixture in the piping bag. Pipe the desired shape.
5. Bake in a preheated oven at 200°C for 10 minutes. Let it cool down to become crisp. Serve.

NOTE

To make spinach puree, grind about ½ cup chopped spinach in a mixer to a puree. Similarly peel and grind beetroot in a mixer to get puree.

Date Fingers

No baking required! Crushed biscuits are mixed with mashed dates, cut into fingers, and rolled in desiccated coconut.

makes 7-8 fingers

Ingredients

- ¾ cup (50 gm) seedless dates (khajur) - chopped
- ¼ cup milk
- 50 gm (6) digestive biscuits - crushed in a mixer
- 4 tbsp desiccated coconut
  (2 tbsp to be used for dusting)
- ½ tsp vanilla essence

Method

1. Pressure cook the dates with milk on high flame to give 1 whistle and switch off the gas. Let the cooker cool completely before opening. The milk will be curdled when you open the cooker, do not worry!
2. In a bowl mix biscuits, 2 tbsp desiccated coconut and essence.
3. Add the steamed dates into the mix and knead to form a dough.
4. Make a 3"x5" block of ¾" thickness on a flat surface. Neaten the edges.
5. Cut into ½" broad fingers. Coat the fingers with the remaining desiccated coconut, covering all the sides completely. Serve.

Oat Ka Halwa

A very healthy sweet treat for the growing children. A good change from the regular suji ka halwa.

serves 2-3

Ingredients
- 1 cup oats - powdered
- 6 tsp of desi ghee (clarified butter)
- ½ cup sugar
- 2 cups water
- 2 chhoti illaichi (green cardamom) - skinned and crushed
- 8-10 kishmish (raisins)
- 8-10 almonds (badam) - cut into thin long pieces

Method
1. Mix water, kishmish, crushed illaichi and sugar. Boil. Remove from fire. Stir to dissolve the sugar. Keep aside.
2. Heat ghee in a kadhai. Fry oats on low heat till they just change colour.
3. Add sugar-water mixture, stirring continuously for 3-4 minutes till the halwa leaves the sides of the kadhai. Remove from fire.
4. Keep in a serving dish. Decorate with shredded almonds. Serve hot.

Caramel Popcorn

Give plain popcorn a sugary, vanilla-scented coating – learn to do this at home the professional way.

serves 2-3

Ingredients

- 1 packet (70 gm) popcorn - (7 cups after popping)
- ½ cup roasted peanuts (moongphali)
- ¾ cup brown sugar
- 3 tsp cornflour dissolved in ¼ cup water
- ¼ tsp salt
- ½ tsp vanilla essence
- ¼ tsp soda-bi-carb (mitha soda)

Method

1. Mix brown sugar, cornflour paste and salt in a big saucepan. Put the pan on fire.
2. Bring to a boil stirring continuously for about 2-3 minutes till it coats the spoon. Remove from fire.
3. Add vanilla essence and soda-bi-carb. Stir.
4. Immediately put popped corns and peanuts. Mix well to coat properly with the caramel.
5. Transfer the popped corns to an oven proof dish.
6. Bake in a pre-heated oven at 250°C for about 8-10 minutes till it has a well browned crispy look.

Atta Laddu

This microwave recipe can make perfect laddus in very little time – so good for the little ones too!

serves 6

Ingredients
- 1 cup whole wheat flour (atta)
- 1/3 cup powdered sugar
- 3-4 tbsp desi ghee
- 1 tbsp dry fruits chopped - (almonds, raisin, pista)
- seeds of 2 green cardamoms (chhoti elaichi) - crushed
- 2 pinches black pepper
- 2 pinches dry ginger powder (saunth), optional

Method
1. Spread atta in a flat dish and microwave for 4 minutes at 80% power to dry roast the wheat flour. Stir once in-between.
2. Add ghee and mix very well. Microwave for 2 minutes at 60% power. Mix well.
3. Microwave for 1½ minutes more at 60% power. Mix well.
4. Add sugar to taste. Add dry fruit and spice powders. Mix very well, make small laddus.

Jam Cookies

The visual appeal of these cookies, along with their sweetly simple taste, makes them a winner with every child.

makes 15

Ingredients

- 240 gm plain flour (maida)
- 1 tsp baking powder
- 140 gm white butter
- 120 gm powdered sugar
- 1 tsp vanilla essence
- ¼-½ cup red jam
- 1 or 2 tbsp milk if needed

Method

1. Sieve flour and baking powder together.
2. Beat butter, sugar and essence with an electric mixer till fluffy. Add flour. Gather together and add milk if mixture is too dry to bind. Mix gently to make a dough. Roll out to 1/8th inch thickness. Cut rounds with the cookie cutter.
3. Cut a hole in the center of 1 round with a tiny round cutter like a cap of an essence bottle. Place this cookie on the cookie without hole. This will form 1 cookie, spoon jam into holes. Use all the dough in the same manner. Bake at 180°C for 15-20 minutes till crisp golden at the edges. Let cookies cool on the baking tray after removing from the oven. Store in a box.

Frozen Chocolate Bananas

Chocolate-coated bananas may not grow on trees – but you can 'grow' them in your freezer with this easy recipe.

serves 6

Ingredients

- 3 bananas - cut each into $\frac{1}{2}$ widthwise to get 2 small pieces
- 6 ice cream sticks
  CHOCOLATE SAUCE
- $\frac{1}{2}$ cup water
- 1 tsp sugar
- 1 tsp butter
- 1 slab (40 gm) chocolate, preferably dark chocolate - softened & cut into small pieces
- 1 tsp cornflour & 1 tsp cocoa - dissolved in $\frac{1}{4}$ cup water

Method

1. Peel and insert a stick in each piece of banana, starting from the cut end and going till halfway.
2. Freeze the bananas in the refrigerator.
3. For the sauce, mix $\frac{1}{2}$ cup water, butter, sugar and chocolate pieces. Bring to a boil on low heat, stirring continuously.
4. Add the dissolved cornflour and cocoa paste. Cook on slow fire for 3-4 minutes, stirring continuously, till the sauce becomes thick and glossy. It should coat the back of the spoon. Remove from fire. Let it cool down.
5. Dip the frozen banana in the chocolate sauce. Coat banana with sauce properly, pouring sauce on the banana with the spoon, if required.
6. Place on a plate. Cover with a plastic wrap or a cling film.
7. Freeze again till both the banana and the sauce turn hard.

Sugar Coated Peanuts

■ Sugar peanuts, an easy snack to make, with raw peanuts, sugar, water, and a little salt.

serves 8

Ingredients
- 1 cup roasted peanuts (moongphali)
- ½ cup sugar
- ¼ cup water

Method
1. In a heavy saucepan add peanuts, sugar and water. Cook on medium heat, stirring, until sugar dissolves and mixture crystallizes and coats peanuts for about 12-15 minutes.
2. Spread peanuts in a plate to cool.

Pineapple Upside Down Cake

This recipe uses condensed milk and aerated soda water for a moist and melting cake that is always popular.

serves 10-12

Ingredients

- ½ tin condensed milk (milkmaid)
- 1¼ cups (125 gm) flour (maida)
- 3/4 tsp baking powder
- 3/4 tsp soda-bicarb
- slightly less than ½ cup (60 gm) salted butter
- ½ cup soda water (aerated soda)
- 1 tsp pineapple essence
- a few drops yellow colour - optional
- 4 tbsp brown sugar
- 4-5 slices (rings) of pineapple - tinned
- a few glace cherries - cut into two pieces
- a few almonds - cut into half

Method

1. Grease an 7" round cake tin. Sprinkle brown sugar to cover the bottom.
2. Drain pineapple rings and cut each into half. Arrange 2 pineapple pieces in the centre & halved pineapple rings on the sides, with a cherry half in the centre of each ring. Place the cherry with the flat, cut side touching the bottom of the tin. Arrange split almonds in between the rings with the flat side touching the bottom of the tin. Keep the decorated tin aside.
3. Melt butter in a pan. Cool. Add milkmaid. Beat well. Add colour & essence.
4. Sieve flour, baking powder & soda-bicarb.
5. Add half of flour & mix well. Add half of the soda to the cake mixture. Beat.
6. Add the left over maida & the aerated soda & beat well.
7. Pour into the decorated cake tin, on top of the pineapple rings. Pat lightly and level with a spatula. Bake in a preheated oven at 150°C/300°F for 30-40 minutes.
8. When the cake is done, remove from oven, loosen sides of the cake and immediately turn onto a plate. (Do not cool in the tin).

Molten Choco Cup Cake

■ These cupcakes are flavoured with orange squash & filled with melted creamy chocolate. Serve warm. Indulge yourself and your youngster's friends!

makes 8 cups

Ingredients

- 175 gm (1¾ cups) flour (maida)
- 1½ tsp baking powder
- ¾ tsp soda-bi-carb
- 1 tbsp less than ½ cup yellow salted butter (60 gm) - softened
- ¾ cup powdered sugar (100 gm)
- ½ cup milk
- ½ cup orange squash or orange crush
  CHOCOLATE FILLING
- ¾ cup (150 gm) cream, preferably Amul cream
- 100 gm dark cooking chocolate - cut into tiny pieces (1 cup)

Method

1. Sieve flour, baking powder and soda-bi-carb.
2. Beat butter and sugar till fluffy.
3. Add half of the flour and half of the milk. Mix well and add the remaining plain flour. Add remaining milk. Beat very well till light and fluffy.
4. Add orange squash or crush and mix to get a soft dropping consistency. Do not beat too much.
5. Line a muffin pan (tray) with paper cups. Spoon mixture into them filling them ¾ only. Bake at 180°C for 25-30 minutes till golden and firm on the top. Keep aside.
6. For filling, heat cream in a small heavy bottomed pan, on low heat (do not boil). Add chocolate and heat stirring continuously for a minute, till chocolate melts and you get a smooth paste. Keep aside to come to room temperature and become slightly thick.
7. Cut out a small circle from the bottom of each muffin. Keep the cap aside. Scoop out the cake slightly. Fill with chocolate filling. Replace the cap again to close the muffin. Keep aside till serving time. Do not refrigerate.
8. To serve, invert the muffins on a serving platter which should be micro-proof. Now you have the muffins with top side up. Warm in a microwave for 10-15 seconds. Serve.

Sweetheart Cookies

Add a fresh taste to these whole wheat cookies with a touch of orange flavouring. Let your kids grow up with good taste!

makes 18

Ingredients
- 1 cup whole wheat flour (atta)
- ½ cup + 2 tbsp butter (50 gms)
- 1 cup powdered sugar
- a few drops orange colour
- ½ tsp orange essence
- ½ tsp baking powder
- a pinch of soda
- 3-4 tsp milk (while kneading if needed)
- 10 almonds - halved

Method
1. Beat butter and sugar until very light and creamy. Add essence and color and beat again.
2. Sieve the flour with baking powder and soda and add to the mixture. Beat again for a few seconds. Add milk if needed to collect into a dough. Knead the dough gently.
3. Roll out dough to ¼" thickness between 2 sheets of polythene. Cut the dough in heart shapes using a biscuit cutter. Decorate the cookies with halved almonds.
4. Put on a greased baking tray and bake the cookies at 180°C for 20 minutes or till light brown on the edges. Remove from oven and let the cookies cool on the baking tray.

Chocolate Biscuit Sticks

■ The batter for these cookies is piped into long sticks using a piping bag – they are baked, cooled, and dipped in melted chocolate.

makes 55-60

Ingredients

- 120 gm whole wheat flour
- 120 gm plain flour (maida)
- 1 tsp baking powder
- 140 gm yellow butter
- 120 gm powdered sugar
- 1 tsp vanilla essence
- ¼ cup + 2 tbsp water

TO COAT

- 100 gm cooking chocolate - melted

Method

1. Sieve both flours & baking powder together.
2. Beat butter, sugar and essence with an electric mixer till fluffy. Add flour. Add ¼ cup water and beat well. Add 2-3 tbsp more water to make a thick, stiff dropping batter which can be piped.
3. Grease a baking sheet or tray with oil. Put the thick batter in a piping bag and pipe long thick fingers.
4. Bake at 160°C for 15-20 minutes till crisp golden at the edges. Let cookies cool on the baking tray after removing from the oven.
5. Melt chocolate on a double boiler and dip about 1/3 of the biscuits in it. Place on a plate lined with aluminium foil. When the chocolate gets set, store in a box.

Peanut Brownies

There are some unusual elements in this recipe which make it a unique, one-of-a-kind brownie. Choose an 8" square tin. A smaller tin would make a higher cake which would remain uncooked inside.

serves 8

Ingredients
- $1\frac{1}{4}$ cups milk (toned)
- 1 tbsp white vinegar
- $1\frac{1}{2}$ cups plain flour (maida)
- $\frac{1}{4}$ cup cocoa
- 1 tsp soda-bi-carb (mitha soda)
- $1\frac{1}{2}$ cups plus 2 tbsp powdered sugar
- $\frac{1}{2}$ cup oil
- 1 tsp vanilla essence
- $\frac{3}{4}$ cup crushed peanuts
- chocolate sauce for decoration
- 8" square tin

Method
1. Boil milk. Add vinegar. When the milk starts to curdle, keep on fire for $\frac{1}{2}$ minute. Remove from fire. Let the paneer cool down to the room temperature. Mash the paneer slightly. Don't separate whey and paneer.
2. Sift plain flour, soda-bi-carb, cocoa and sugar and mix well with the spoon. Add $\frac{1}{2}$ cup crushed peanuts to the flour mix.
3. Put the flour ingredients in a mixing bowl.
4. Add oil and the paneer alongwith the water (whey). Add essence. Mix well with a wooden spoon.
5. Grease an 8 inches square baking tin. Line with paper and grease paper. Transfer cake mix in the tin.
6. Sprinkle $\frac{1}{4}$ cup crushed peanuts and bake at 160°C for 40 minutes.
7. Remove from oven. Let it cool down completely in the tin. Cut into squares in the tin. Remove brownie pieces from tin. To serve, top with chocolate sauce if you like.

Fruit and Jelly Wedges
■ Set the jelly in hollowed out orange shells for an attractive look.

makes 8

Ingredients
- ½ packet ready-made jelly
- 3 tbsp - chopped raisins (kishmish)
- 2 tbsp - chopped almonds (badam)
- 2 large oranges

Method
1. Make jelly as given on the packet but reduce the water by ½ cup.
2. Add nuts and refrigerate until mixture just begins to thicken.
3. Cut oranges in half and scoop out the pulp with the help of a spoon. Fill the jelly mixture into orange shells. Place shells on a tray and refrigerate for 2-3 hours or until jelly is set.
4. To serve, cut each jelly filled shell into two wedges.

NOTE
The orange pulp can be churned in a mixer to get juice for the child. Remember to remove the seeds.

Fresh Fruit Kebabs
■ An elegant presentation to make the kids feel like grown ups!

makes 6

Ingredients
- 6 strawberries - cut into halves if big
- 1 kiwi - cut into cubes
- 12 green grapes
- 12 black grapes
- 1 apple - cut into cubes
- 1 orange - segmented & cut into cubes
- 6 bamboo skewers
  MARINADE
- juice of ½ lemon
- 2 tbsp honey

Method
1. Mix the ingredients of marinade and put all the fruits in it. Keep in the fridge for ½ hour.
2. Skewer the fruit alternating one after the other on to the bamboo skewers (see picture) and serve.

NOTE
You can use any fruit of your choice.

Donuts

The detailed steps explained in this recipe will help you to make doughnuts that have the right light texture.

makes 8 medium

Ingredients

- 200 gm flour
- 15 gm fresh yeast or 2 tsp dry yeast
- 2 tbsp sugar
- 1 egg, optional
- 15 gm nestle milk powder
- 40 gm yellow butter
- $\frac{1}{2}$ tsp improver, optional
- 100 ml water, approx.
- 1 tsp vanilla essence

Method

1. Mix maida, improver and milk powder in a big parat. Run in the butter lightly with fingers. Keep aside.
2. Warm 100 ml water. Put in a bowl. Add sugar and mix with a spoon. Add yeast and shake gently to mix. Cover the bowl and rest the yeast for 5-7 minutes in a warm closed place for 5 minutes to bubble and activate.
3. Make a well in the maida in a parat or on a work surface. Add yeast. Add egg and essence. and mix using a rubber spatula for mixing. Mix well with hands for 4-5 minutes till it stops being sticky. Make a soft dough which is not too sticky by beating the dough well on the work surface. Rub hands with oil and make a nice ball and place on a plate. Cover the plate with wrap and let dough rest for 20-30 minutes in a closed place.
4. Dust the work surface with flour. Make 8 balls. Roll out each ball of dough lightly to about $\frac{1}{4}$" thick. With the back of a nozzle cut the centre also to get the hole, or you can use a donut cutter.
5. Dust a tray with flour (donuts stick otherwise).
6. Place on the dusted tray and cover tray with wrap. Keep aside.
7. Heat oil in a kadhai till slightly hot. Do not heat too much.
8. Add 1 doughnut and check. Let it not brown quickly. Put 5-6 donuts in oil together and fry on very low heat till very light golden. Remove from oil and put on a absorbent paper to remove excess oil.

NOTE

Bread improver is available in the market, though not very easily. It helps to improve the texture of donuts/breads.

Choco Cake

Any family celebration can be the occasion to make this gorgeous chocolate cake smothered in an equally gorgeous chocolate icing.

serves 12

Ingredients

- ½ tin condensed milk (milk-maid)
- 100 gms (1 cup) maida
- ¼ cup cocoa, ½ tsp level soda-bicarb
- 1 tsp level baking powder
- ½ cup oil, 3 tbsp powdered sugar
- ½ cup milk, approx.
- 1½ tsp vanilla essence
- a baking tin of 7" diameter, see note
- brown paper to line

TRUFFLE ICING

- 200 gms cream, preferably amul
- 300 gms dark cooking chocolate - chipped (3 cups)

Method

1. Line the bottom of a round cake tin with brown paper. Grease the paper and the sides.
2. Sift maida with cocoa, soda-bicarb and baking powder. Keep aside.
3. Beat milk maid. Gradually add sugar and beat till fluffy.
4. Add oil. Beat well.
5. Add half the maida. Mix. Add half of the milk. Beat well. Add essence.
6. Add the remaining maida and the milk beating well after the addition. Beat well for 3-4 minutes till the mixture is smooth and light and a thick pouring ribbon consistency.
7. Put the mixture in the tin. Bake for 40 minutes in a preheated oven at 150°C.
8. To make truffle icing, heat 100 gms cream in a heavy bottom pan on low heat till it becomes hot. Do not let it boil. Add 150 gms chocolate to it. Mix nicely to remove any lumps. Remove from fire when almost melted and mix well. Let it cool to room temperature.
9. Keep cake on a rack. Place a plate under the rack.
10. Pour the prepared icing on the set cake and tilt it to cover the sides also. The truffle icing can be reheated with 1-2 tbsp water, if it has become extra thick. It should be thin enough to flow properly.

NOTE

You can also put this truffle icing on marie biscuits. Children love it!

Nan Khatai

A soft dough, flavoured with cardamom, is formed into balls then baked. The combination of baking powder and baking soda creates the typical airy texture.

Makes 30-35 pieces

Ingredients
- 250 gm (2½ cups) flour (maida)
- 1 cup powdered sugar
- 150 gm (1 cup) desi ghee
- ¼ tsp baking soda (mitha soda)
- ¼ tsp baking powder
- 2 tsp curd - beat till smooth
- a pinch of salt
- ¼ tsp green cardamom (elaichi) powder

Method
1. Sift flour with baking soda and keep aside.
2. Beat ghee with baking powder till very soft and fluffy.
3. Add sugar gradually. Beat till very fluffy. Add salt, cardamom and curd.
4. Add flour. Mix with a spoon. Knead lightly. Add 2-3 tbsp water for a smooth soft dough.
5. Make balls. Flatten balls. Sprinkle cardamom powder. Give shallow cross-cuts. Bake at 160°C for 20-25 minutes till edges turn golden.

Fruity Chocolate Squares

These chilled morsels have crushed biscuits, raisins and thick luscious chocolate; they can be decorated with any seasonal fruit – gourmet class but so easy to make!

serves 10

Ingredients

- 200 gm marie biscuits (crushed into very tiny pieces)
- ¼ cup black raisins (kishmish)
- 200 gm cooking chocolate - cut into small pieces
- 100 gm cream
- ½ tsp vanilla essence
- 3-4 strawberries or 1 kiwi

Method

1. Crush biscuits and mix essence with it. Add raisins.
2. Heat cream on very low heat in a heavy-bottomed pan. Add chocolate pieces to it. Mix it well till chocolate melts. Remove from fire and stir well to make a smooth sauce.
3. Mix a little more than half of the sauce with the crushed biscuits, just enough to bind the mixture nicely.
4. Line a loaf tin with aluminium foil and put the mixture into it. Press and level it with your hands. Keep in the freezer for 10 minutes till set.
5. Demould the set biscuits on a wire rack. Place a plate underneath the rack. Heat the remaining sauce, if need be with a tbsp of water and pour on the set biscuit mixture. Level the sauce on the sides with palatte knife and keep it back in the fridge for 10-15 minutes to set.
6. Cut into 2" square pieces and decorate it with any sliced of fresh fruit of your choice and serve chilled.

Jelly Custard

You need to start the preparation about 5 hours before you want to serve this dessert, as the jelly needs time to set. We have used strawberry jelly but any flavour would be great, so choose your favourite!

serves 4

Ingredients

- 5½ tbsp custard powder
- 5 tbsp sugar
- 2½ cups milk
- 2 cups boiling water
- 1 packet (90 gms) strawberry jelly crystals

FOR DECORATING
- strawberries, gems or any candies etc.

Method

1. Mix custard powder, sugar and ½ cup milk in a bowl.
2. Heat rest of the milk. Add dissolved custard, stirring well. Stir the custard until it boils and becomes thicker for 7-8 minutes on medium heat. Keep aside to cool.
3. Boil 2 cups water. Remove from fire. Sprinkle jelly and stir until the crystals are dissolved and the mixture is clear.
4. Take 4 serving glasses/bowls or a serving dish. Pour the jelly evenly into the glasses/bowls. Set in the freezer for 10-20 minutes till semiset.
5. Whip prepared custard then pour it slowly over the jelly. Cover each with platic wrap and put the glasses in the refrigerator for about 4 hours or until the jelly is set.
6. Just before serving, decorate the tops with the strawberries/jems or sprinklers etc.

Cinnamon Wheat Crispies

■ Aniseed and cinnamon bring an exotic touch to these dainty, easy-to-make cookies – no oven required!

makes 50

Ingredients
- 1 cup atta
- 1 cup plain flour (maida)
- ¼ cup olive oil
- ½ tsp ground aniseed (saunf)
- 1 tsp ground cinnamon (dalchini)
- ½ cup sugar syrup
- oil for frying
- some powdered sugar for dusting

TO DUST
- 2 tbsp icing sugar
- ½ tsp ground cinnamon (dalchini)

Method

1. Whisk oil with aniseeds, cinnamon and sugar syrup. Keep aside.
2. Place 2 cups flour in a food processor, holding back a few spoonfuls. With motor running, add the liquid mixture. The dough will be softish. If it is too soft to handle, add the extra flour. Turn on to a worksurface and knead for 3-4 minutes until smooth and elastic. Cover and rest at room temperature for 30 minutes. Roll out the dough very thinly between 2 plastic sheets, dusting with a little extra flour if necessary. Cut with a knife or a pizza cutter into diamond shape or star shape or any other shape. Sprinkle powdered sugar. Prick with a fork.
3. Deep-fry 6-8 at a time, on low heat for 5-6 minutes till golden and crisp. Drain from oil. Sprinkle sifted icing sugar and cinnamon or flick with warmed honey.

TO MAKE SUGAR SYRUP

Boil ½ cup water with 4 tbsp sugar. Simmer on low heat for 3-4 minutes till slightly thick, of juice consistency.

Shakes & Ice cream

Teenagers seem to be hungry all the time - a sign of the growth spurt they are experiencing. The recipes in this chapter will show you innovative shakes and ice creams which don't take you all day to make, and are a big hit with the children!

Yogurt Pops

What a wonderful list of ingredients, balanced between nutrition and popularity. A simple, one-step method and a result that brings smiles all around.

makes 7

Ingredients

CHURN TOGETHER IN A MIXER
- ½ cup yogurt (curd) - hang in a muslin cloth for 15 minutes
- ¼ cup grapes (green or black)
- ¼ cup chopped strawberries
- 4 tbsp orange squash
- 4 tbsp coke or any cola drink
- 5 dry apricots (khumani) - chopped or 1 tbsp raisins
- 3 tbsp sugar, or to taste

Method

1. Churn all the ingredients together in a mixer. Pour mixture into ice-block (ice-lolly) moulds or ice cube trays, cover loosely with plastic food wrap and freeze for 5 hours or until solid. Serve.

Mango Duet Ice Cream

A double shade of yellow adds pizzazz to these homemade popsicles to store in your freezer. They need a day to set so plan ahead.

makes 8

Ingredients
- 2 cups ready-made mango juice
- 1/3 cup sugar
- 1 cup water
- ½ cup cream
- kulfi or popsicle moulds

Method
1. Cook 1/3 cup sugar and 1 cup water in a sauce pan on medium heat stirring until the sugar is dissolved and the mixture is clear. Stop stirring and simmer on low heat without a lid, for 12-15 minutes till it becomes ½ cup.
2. Carefully pour the sugar mixture into a cup. It should measure ½ cup (If you have too much liquid, cook it for a bit longer. If you have too little, add enough water to make ½ cup).
3. Whisk mango juice with the cooled sugar syrup.
4. Put cream into a bowl. Add ½ cup of the mango-syrup mixture to the cream.
5. Keep the remaining mango mixture in another bowl.
6. Pour the cream mango mixture into the moulds filling them upto ¾ part of the mould. Freeze them for 1½ hours or until the pops start to set. Take the pops out of the freezer and push a stick into each if needed.
7. Pour the other mango mix into the moulds on top to fill. Return the pops to the freezer overnight so they are frozen solid.

Apricot Almond Delight

■ The delicate flavour and interesting texture of juicy apricots and almonds complement each other beautifully in this light and fluffy drink.

serves 2

Ingredients
- 10 pieces of dried apricots (100 gm)
- 1 cup milk
- 1½ tbsp sugar
- ½ tsp almond or vanilla essence
- ½ tbsp finely chopped almonds

Method
1. Place apricots in a bowl, pour in sufficient water to cover and leave to soak for atleast 3-4 hours or overnight.
2. Drain apricots & place in a food processor or blender with milk, sugar & almond essence. Process until smooth.
3. Pour into individual glasses. Refrigerate until firm.
4. To serve sprinkle with chopped almonds.

Orange Yogurt Ice Cream

A yogurt ice cream that is so professional – it is hard to believe it is completely home made.

serves 6

Ingredients

- 5 cups full-cream milk
- 6 tbsp skimmed milk powder
- ½ cup sugar
- 2 tsp gelatine, 3 tbsp water
- 400 gm yogurt, ready made
- 5 tbsp powdered sugar
- few drops orange colour
- 2 tsp orange essence
- ½ tsp vanilla essence
- few glaced cherries - cut into fine pieces, optional

Method

1. Dissolve milk powder in ½ cup warm milk and keep aside. Strain the milk powder paste into the leftover 4½ cups milk. Add sugar. Boil milk, stirring occasionally.
2. Keep on medium flame for 25 minutes after the first boil. Adjust the flame so as to keep the milk boiling slowly all the time. Stir frequently to prevent the milk from boiling over.
3. Dissolve gelatine in 2 tbsp water on low flame in a heavy bottomed pan and keep aside.
4. After the milk has been on fire for 25 minutes, add the gelatine solution to the milk, stirring continuously. Cook for 1 minute more on very low heat. Do not let it boil. Remove from fire. Cool. Cover well and freeze for 4-5 hours or overnight, or till set.
5. When the milk has frozen, hang the yogurt in a muslin cloth for ½ hour. Squeeze gently to remove any excess liquid. Beat hung yogurt with sugar and both the essences till smooth.
6. Cut frozen milk into small pieces. Beat till fluffy. Mix the hung yogurt in it. Add colour.
7. Transfer to an ice cream box. Sprinkle cherries on the ice cream. Mix gently. Cover nicely with a cling wrap first and then with the lid of the box and freeze till firm. Serve.
8. You can also beat it once again after 2-3 hours when it is almost set, for a fluffier yogurt. Freeze again till firm.

Fresh Chikoo Ice Cream

Fresh, pureed chikoos, and fresh, whipped cream are bound with dissolved gelatine – no cooking required for this pure and simple chikoo delight.

serves 4

Ingredients
- 200-250 gm fresh ripe chikoo
- 250 gm fresh cream
- 6 tbsp powdered sugar
- 1 tsp gelatine
- ½ tsp vanilla essence
- 2 tbsp kishmish, preferably black raisins

Method
1. Peel the chikoo and chop. Grind to a puree.
2. Soak gelatine in 1 tbsp water in a small pan for 5 minutes. Stir on low heat till it dissolves.
3. Add gelatine to chikoo puree and mix well.
4. Whip cream with powdered sugar till thick.
5. Add chikoo puree to whipped cream. Mix well. Add essence and raisins. Mix and check sugar.
6. Transfer to an ice cream box. Cover with a plastic sheet (cling wrap) and then with the lid. Freeze overnight or till firm.

Kesar Badam Milk

Froth up some saffron-flavoured milk in a blender then whip in some ice cream – a super-duper 'glass of milk' for your child.

serves 2

Ingredients
- 500 ml (3 cups) milk
- 3 tbsp sugar
- 2 large scoops of vanilla ice cream
- a few drops of yellow colour - optional
- 10-15 almonds (badam)
- a few strands of saffron (kesar)

Method
1. Soak kesar in 2-3 tbsp warm milk for 5-7 minutes. Rub the soaked kesar with a spoon to extract colour and flavour.
2. Boil rest of the milk with sugar and the dissolved kesar. Keep on low flame for 5 minutes. Cool. Chill.
3. Powder almonds coarsely.
4. Blend chilled kesar milk with powdered almonds and yellow colour in a blender for a few seconds till frothy.
5. Add ice cream and whip for another second. Serve.

Mango Mania

Fresh mango pulp and fresh whipped cream are bound with dissolved gelatine – no cooking required for this pure and simple mango delight.

serves 6

Ingredients
- 2 ripe mangoes
- 250 gm fresh cream
- 5 tbsp powdered sugar
- a few drops yellow colour
- 1 tsp gelatine

Method
1. Blend mangoes to a puree in a mixer to get about 2 cups puree.
2. Soak gelatine in 1 tbsp water for about 2-3 minutes. Cook on low heat till it dissolves.
3. Add gelatine to mango puree and mix well.
4. Whip chilled cream with powdered sugar till thick.
5. Add mango puree and mix well.
6. Add colour if required. Check sugar.
7. Transfer to an ice cream box. Cover with a plastic sheet (cling wrap) and then with the lid. Freeze overnight or till firm.

Orange Rose Smoothie

■ Lightly frothy and filled with natural goodness. This creamy orange smoothie takes just a few ingredients, but makes a wholesome morning drink!

serves 1

Ingredients
- ½ cup vanilla soya milk
- ½ cup orange juice
- 1 tbsp rooh afza, 5 ice cubes
- 2 tsp sugar, ¼ tsp vanilla extract

Method
1. In a blender combine all the ingredients. Cover and process for 30 to 40 seconds or until smooth.
2. Pour into chilled glasses. Serve immediately.

Breakfast Smoothie

■ Frozen yogurt, fresh fruit and nuts are the base of this breakfast smoothie.

serves 2

Ingredients
- 1 cup chopped soft ripe fruit (strawberry/water melon/peach/mango)
- ½ cup milk
- ¼ cup chilled/frozen yogurt
- 2 tbsp roasted oats/muesili
- 1 tbsp chopped almonds/walnuts
- 2 tbsp sugar or sugar free to taste
- 1-2 drops vanilla essence

Method
1. In a blender combine all the ingredients. Cover & process for 30 to 40 seconds or until smooth.
2. Pour into chilled glasses. Serve immediately.

Nutty Banana Smoothie

■ Kids of all ages will enjoy this orange-banana smoothie flavoured with honey and nuts.

serves 1

Ingredients
- 1 cup orange juice
- 1 frozen medium banana - cut into pieces
- 1 tsp peanuts - roughly crushed
- 1-2 tbsp honey

Method
1. Pour orange juice into blender.
2. Add banana, peanuts and honey and blend until smooth. Pour in a glass and serve.

Strawberry Smoothie

■ Fresh strawberries and strawberry crush whisked with yogurt in a quick and easy recipe.

serves 1

Ingredients
- $\frac{1}{4}$ cup yogurt
- 2 strawberries
- 2 tbsp strawberry crush
- 1-2 tsp honey
- 2 pinches cinnamon
- $\frac{1}{2}$ cup cold water
- 2-3 ice cube

Method
1. Grind strawberries in a grinder to a puree. Transfer to a blender. Add other ingredients and blend well.

INTERNATIONAL CONVERSION GUIDE
These are not exact equivalents; they've been rounded-off to make measuring easier.

Weights & Measures

Metric	Imperial
15 g	½ oz
30 g	1 oz
60 g	2 oz
90 g	3 oz
125 g	4 oz (¼ lb)
155 g	5 oz
185 g	6 oz
220 g	7 oz
250 g	8 oz (½ lb)
280 g	9 oz
315 g	10 oz
345 g	11 oz
375 g	12 oz (¾ lb)
410 g	13 oz
440 g	14 oz
470 g	15 oz
500 g	16 oz (1 lb)
750 g	24 oz (1½ lb)
1 kg	30 oz (2 lb)

Liquid Measures

Metric	Imperial
30 ml	1 fluid oz
60 ml	2 fluid oz
100 ml	3 fluid oz
125 ml	4 fluid oz
150 ml	5 fluid oz (¼ pint/1 gill)
190 ml	6 fluid oz
250 ml	8 fluid oz
300 ml	10 fluid oz (½ pint)
500 ml	16 fluid oz
600 ml	20 fluid oz (1 pint)
1000 ml	1¾ pints

Cups & Spoon Measures

Metric	Imperial
1 ml	¼ tsp
2 ml	½ tsp
5 ml	1 tsp
15 ml	1 tbsp
60 ml	¼ cup
125 ml	½ cup
250 ml	1 cup

Helpful Measures

Metric	Imperial
3 mm	1/8 in
6 mm	¼ in
1 cm	½ in
2 cm	¾ in
2.5 cm	1 in
5 cm	2 in
6 cm	2½ in
8 cm	3 in
10 cm	4 in
13 cm	5 in
15 cm	6 in
18 cm	7 in
20 cm	8 in
23 cm	9 in
25 cm	10 in
28 cm	11 in
30 cm	12 in (1ft)

HOW TO MEASURE
When using the graduated metric measuring cups, it is important to shake the dry ingredients loosely into the required cup. Do not tap the cup on the table, or pack the ingredients into the cup unless otherwise directed. Level top of cup with a knife. When using graduated metric measuring spoons, level top of spoon with a knife. When measuring liquids in the jug, place jug on a flat surface, check for accuracy at eye level.

OVEN TEMPERATURE
These oven temperatures are only a guide. Always check the manufacturer's manual.

	°C (Celsius)	°F (Fahrenheit)	Gas Mark
Very low	120	250	1
Low	150	300	2
Moderately low	160	325	3
Moderate	180	350	4
Moderately high	190	375	5
High	200	400	6
Very high	230	450	7

Herbs & Spices

ENGLISH NAME	HINDI NAME
1 Asafoetida	1 Hing
2 Bay Leaves	2 Tej Patta
3 Cardamom	3 Elaichi, Chhoti Elaichi
4 Cardamom, Black	4 Moti Elaichi
5 Carom Seeds	5 Ajwain
6 Chillies, Green	6 Hari Mirch
7 Chillies, Dry Red	7 Sukhi Sabut Lal Mirch
8 Chilli Powder, Red	8 Lal Mirch Powder
9 Cinnamon	9 Dalchini
10 Cloves	10 Laung
11 Coriander Seeds	11 Sabut Dhania
12 Coriander Seeds, ground	12 Dhania Powder
13 Coriander Leaves	13 Hara Dhania
14 Cumin Seeds	14 Jeera
15 Cumin Seeds, black	15 Shah Jeera
16 Curry Leaves	16 Kari Patta
17 Fennel Seeds	17 Saunf
18 Fenugreek Seeds	18 Methi Dana
19 Fenugreek Leaves, Dried	19 Kasuri Methi
20 Garam Masala Powder	20 Garam Masala
21 Garlic	21 Lahsun
22 Ginger	22 Adrak
23 Mace	23 Javitri
24 Mango Powder, Dried	24 Amchur
25 Melon Seeds	25 Magaz
26 Mint Leaves	26 Pudina
27 Mustard Seeds	27 Rai, Sarson
28 Nigella, Onion Seeds	28 Kalaunji
29 Nutmeg	29 Jaiphal
30 Peppercorns	30 Sabut Kali Mirch
31 Pomegranate Seeds, Dried	31 Anardana
32 Sesame Seeds	32 Til
33 Saffron	33 Kesar
34 Turmeric Powder	34 Haldi

FREE HOME DELIVERY OF NITA MEHTA BOOKS
Call: 011-23250091, 23252948 (within India)

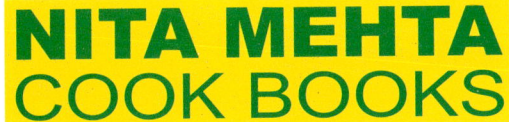
India's No.1 Cookbooks

Enriching Young Minds

NITA MEHTA COOKERY CLUB

Become a

Get  Books

buy online at: www.nitamehta.com

NITA MEHTA STORY BOOKS
Enriching Young Minds

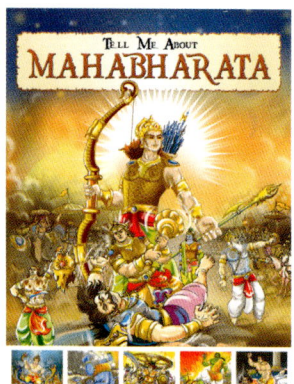
Tell me about Mahabharata

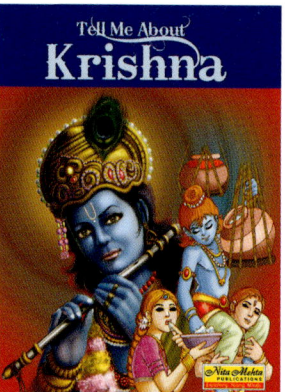
Tell me about Krishna

Tell me about Sikh Gurus

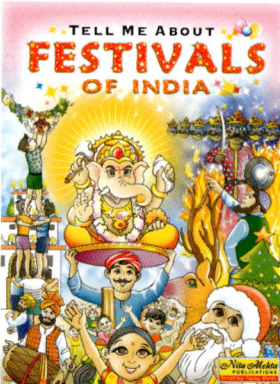
Tell me about Festivals

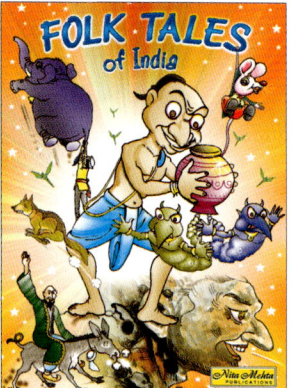
Folk Tales of India

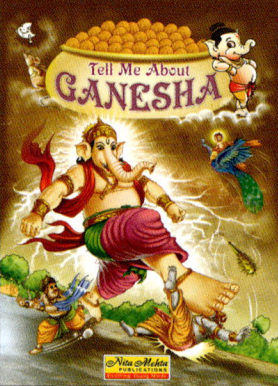
Tell me about Ganesha

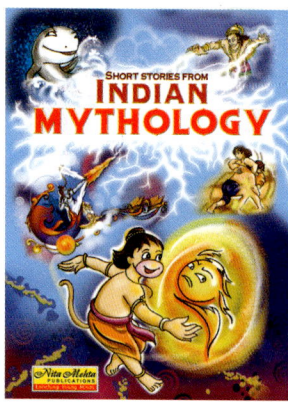
Short Stories from Indian Mythology

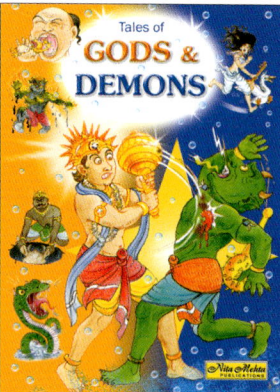
Tales of Gods & Demons

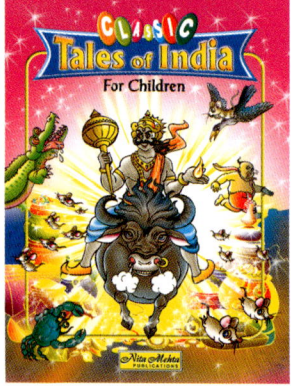
Classic Tales of India

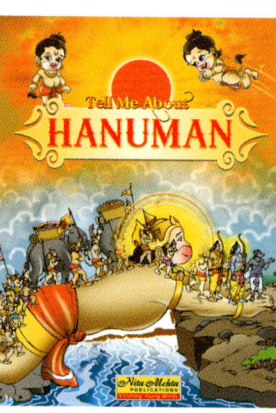
Tell me about Hanuman

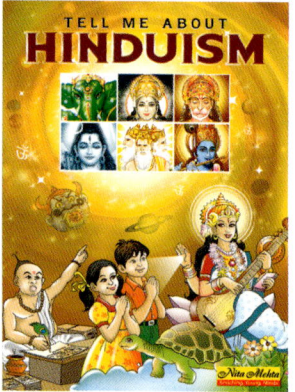
Tell me about Hinduism

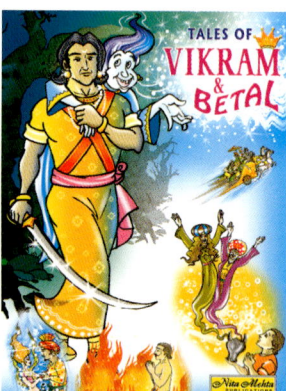
Tales of Vikram & Betal

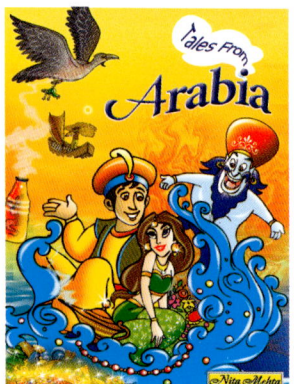
Tales from Arabia

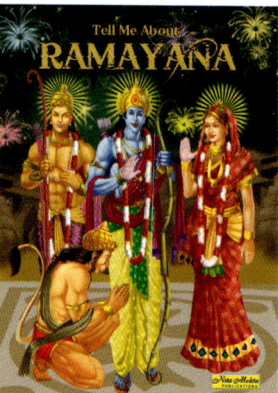
Tell me about Ramayana

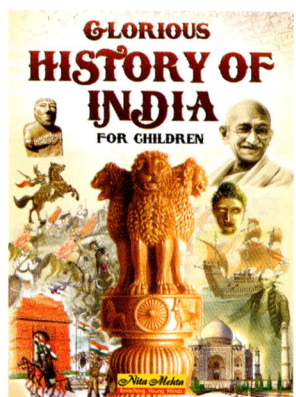
Glorious History of India

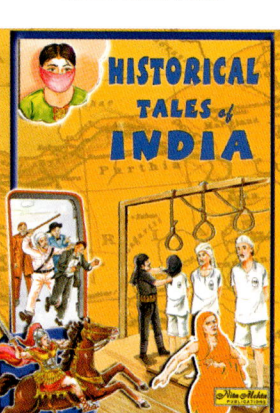
Historical Tales of India